THE FLYTIER'S CRAFT

THE
FLYTIER'S CRAFT
A Practical Guide

Mike Shanks

SWAN·HILL
PRESS

Front Cover Photograph

This fly has no name, neither does it need one. There are more than enough artificial fly names already.

It is impractical in terms of the materials used, the time it takes to tie and its negative fishing qualities. It merely represents a style of salmon fly designed to catch the angler rather than the fish.

First published in the UK in 1992
by Swan Hill Press
an imprint of Airlife Publishing Ltd.

British Library Cataloguing in Publication Data
A catalogue record is available for this book
from the British Library

ISBN 1 85310 237 7

Printed by Livesey Ltd., Shrewsbury, England.

Swan Hill Press

An imprint of Airlife Publishing Ltd.
101 Longden Road, Shrewsbury SY3 9EB.

Contents

Acknowledgements

I am very grateful to my wife Janet for her moral support and the many hours she has spent deciphering my lousy handwriting and toiling over a hot word processor.

Grateful thanks are also due to Leslie Colville for his tireless efforts with the camera.

Thanks to all the anglers and flytiers, too numerous to mention, whose ideas and help have contributed to the writing of this book.

List of Plates

Preface

Flytying is a craft. It is the use of a limited set of skills to produce a functional object. Few flytiers, once they have mastered the basics, are content simply to copy the ideas of others. The vast majority of us are constantly making small alterations in the hope of creating more successful patterns. Only a very few tiers are truly creative artists. I do not count myself in this group.

The reader of this book will find a comprehensive range of techniques sufficient to tie every pattern which he/she is likely to see. The majority of techniques and fly types are illustrated with clear diagrams and plates. Perhaps even more important he/she will find encouragement to experiment. Throughout, the text refers to a wide variety of artificial flies, many of which are to be found on the plates. The patterns for all these flies are included in the appendix. In particular the rationale for my SB style of fly, which is mentioned regularly will be found in Part Two.

There is nothing quite like catching a fish on a fly you have tied yourself. If the fly incorporates an idea of your own, so much the better. No craftsman can be completely satisfied with a product which does not contain a little of himself.

The nice thing about experimenting is that every fly will work on its day and no matter what theory we come up with for success or failure none of these can be proved. Being dogmatic about anything in angling is futile.

Part One

FLY
CONSTRUCTION

1 Introduction

Before beginning the detailed description of how to tie individual parts of a fly, there are some basic points to consider. If we begin with the right approach many of the physical details will come with surprising ease.

To begin with, all the directions assume that the hook has been placed in the vice so that the shank is horizontal. There are some exceptions of course. A grub hook for example does not have a straight shank. I prefer this type of hook for my SB trout patterns (Plate 2). However, although unusual hooks can be useful for certain flies, there are a few occasions when they are vital.

If we are to use a normal straight-shanked hook there are two possible ways of holding it in the vice, whichever you use is simply a matter of preference.

In the first (Figure 1.1) very little of the hook is gripped in the jaws of the vice. The main advantage of this is that the point and barb are visible to use as reference points for tags, tails and bodies. In the second (Figure 1.2) more of the hook is gripped. With the point of the hook covered there is no chance of cutting the tying thread on the point. With experience it should be possible to judge accurately the proportions without seeing point and barb.

It is of course possible to abandon the vice altogether. There are those flytiers who will tell you that a vice is not necessary — they are right. However, never believe anyone who tells you that it is a sign of skill to do without one. Holding a hook between finger and thumb has only one

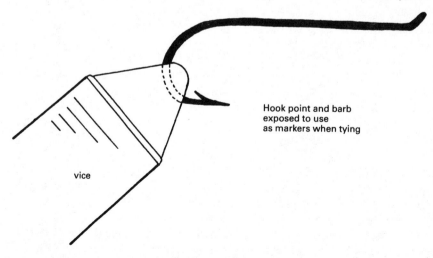

vice

Hook point and barb
exposed to use
as markers when tying

Figure 1.1. Very little of the hook is gripped.

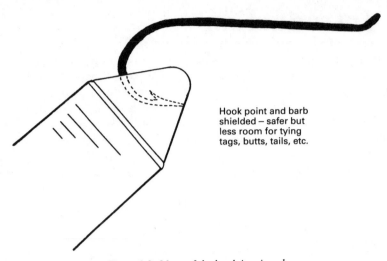

Figure 1.2. More of the hook is gripped.

advantage — being able to quickly see both sides of the hook to check that both sides of the fly are balanced and symmetrical. There are so many disadvantages in not using a vice which makes the vice essential in my opinion, so don't handicap yourself. The vice doesn't need to be too elaborate: I started with a pair of pliers held closed with a strong elastic band and gripped between the knees. Not very comfortable but it did work.

The number of turns of thread needed to hold each part of the fly may not always be given. Different materials require different treatment depending on how coarse they may be or how strong the thread is. Holding on fine materials such as floss silk may require no turns at all until the next material is fixed (see Figure 1.4). A large bunch of bucktail may require many turns to secure it properly. However, if the number is not specified the rule of thumb is this: use as few as you can get away with; this helps neatness especially on the smaller trout flies.

Looking back at some of my early efforts at flytying I am able to identify the reasons why they were inadequate both in construction and attractiveness to fish. *Too much*, are the words which immediately spring to mind. Every part of every dressing was overdone. This is always a mistake.

A potter once told me that the best pots were those with the least possible turning on the wheel. The same philosophy can be equally applied to flytying. Beginners, and some others, often seem to have the idea that a hackle is wasted if every possible turn is not extracted from it. This is false. Where fur bodies are concerned, decided what is an appropriate amount to use, then put at least half of it back in its packet before dubbing, you will still have more than enough.

Shop-bought flies of every type are nearly always over-dressed. Price, it seems, depends on quantity of material rather than quality of tying. Possibly too many of these are made by non-anglers.

The suggestions and ideas to be found in the following pages are in no way intended to be definitive. Quite simply they are methods which have served me very well for both fishing and competition purposes. Both should have basically the same principles, except that neatness is normally well down the list of priorities for fishing, but at the top of the list for competitions. Having absorbed a great deal of flytying literature, words of wisdom, practical hints, useful theories — and some utter guff — I have gathered and developed for myself a series of procedures which suit my own style and needs.

For my own satisfaction I must have a legitimate reason for every aspect of construction. This requires careful thought about what I expect a fly to do in or on the water. Some standard ideas I have retained for some flies and rejected for others. There are many similarities between the appearance of flies used for different species of fish which may have very different types of behaviour. Wet flies for brown trout, sea trout and salmon often differ from one another only in size. Yet the probable reasons for each of these fish taking a fly are quite different. Therefore, there is no reason why the construction of flies for these three fish should be the same.

There is an almost infinite number of tying methods and materials at our disposal, despite the ever-increasing banned list. Experimentation both in materials and construction is what makes flytying such a fascinating pastime.

After tying several patterns I am often left with a few oddments which are thrown hurriedly onto a hook rather than into the bin. Usually they are given away or stuck in my hat to be given one chance. It is amazing just how successful these oddities can be. They spawn ideas for new flies or variations on the old. One noteworthy example was constructed from a few trimmings of dyed red squirrel tail. This was chopped up and dubbed into a shaggy body and ribbed with a scrap of wire. That was all. It became a useful loch pattern, early one season, for a friend who caught fish while I draw blanks on tried and trusted patterns.

Never blindly follow anyone else's patterns. Their purpose or method of fishing may not be exactly the same as your own. For every method or material we should always ask ourselves two questions:

1   Does this perfectly fulfil the purpose which I require?
2   How important could it be to the fish in terms of appearance, mobility, translucency, etc?

Both of these are often equally important, especially with non-representative patterns.

Try to think out every detail before you begin. It will help to choose materials of appropriate colour, texture and so on. In turn these may have a bearing on proportion and methods used. It is always useful to have a clear impression of the finished product rather than concentrating on each item in turn.

2 Hooks, Threads and Tools

There is no point at all in spending time and effort tying a good dressing over a poor hook except for practice. Obvious as this advice ought to be, it is not always followed. A soft or brittle hook is useless and tackle shops are full of them. Partridge are the best that I have found because they are the most consistently well made (Figure 2.1).

More has been written with less general agreement on hooks than on any other aspect of flies. Should the point be needle sharp or very slightly blunted? Which type of bend is best for strength? Should the hook be forged or not? Are singles, doubles or trebles the best for sea trout or salmon flies? There are many conflicting ideas about all these and other questions, but none can be proved beyond all doubt.

A hook is more than a device for holding a fish. The curvature of the wire may produce a more realistic foundation for the bodies of some flies. The shape of the hook may add realism to the fly but this must never be allowed to compromise hooking ability. A grub hook is a good example of a good mixture of the two. There are grounds for doubting the value of some other designs but you must decide for yourself.

Basic Selection of Hooks

There is a huge range of hook styles, many designed for a specific type of fly. It would be impossible for the average angler/flytier to amass all of these. Neither is there any need to possess them all because with a small range all types of fly or lure for all types of fish can be constructed effectively. What follows is my own basic choice and includes relevant Partridge code numbers.

1 *Down eye, wide gape, code A*
   This hook has a shorter than standard shank which is ideal for spiders, nymphs, sedge and midge pupae. I also prefer it to other hooks for some Palmer-style flies.
2 *Down eye, Sproat bend, code G3A; or Down eye, Captain Hamilton, code L1A–L4A*
   Either of these are better for most winged wet fly patterns as they have a standard length shank. They are good general purpose hooks for many wet patterns, even some nymphs and lures.

   The Captain Hamilton option has an advantage over Sproat bends in that they may be obtained in different gauges of wire which you may find useful depending on the sinking rate you require of a fly.

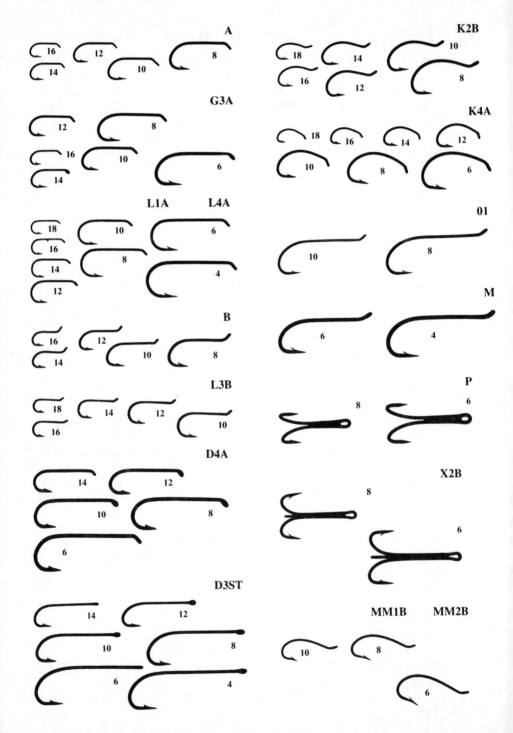

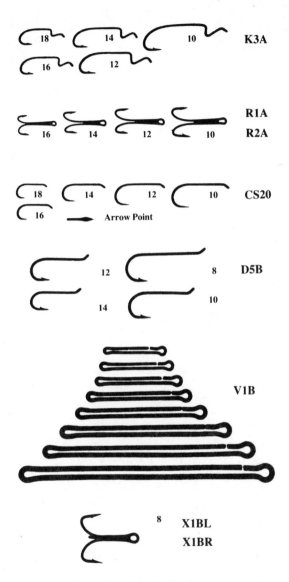

Figure 2.1. Partridge hook types.

3 *Up eye, wind gape, code B dry fly hook; or Up eye, Captain Hamilton,*
code L3B dry fly hook
Either is perfect for nearly all types of dry flies. I also use up eye hooks
for the tail hook of some tandems — sunk lures and secret weapons. Up
eye hooks are better than down eye if the gap between the hooks is to
be as small as possible, to avoid tangling.

4   *Long shank hooks, Bucktail Streamer hook, code D4A; or Straight eye lure hooks, code D3ST*
    Used for all kinds of lures for rainbow, brown and sea trout, even some low-water style flies. Some naturals are also better tied on long shank hooks: stick flies, wet Mayflies and nymphs and sedges on smaller sizes.
5   *Caddis/grub hooks, code K2B or K4A*
    These are used for representations of naturals which have a pronounced curve in their bodies: hatching sedges, midges, freshwater shrimps and SBs.
6   *Wilson dry fly hooks, code 01*
    These are perfect for sea trout flies in the Medicine style, low-water salmon flies and even trout lures.
7   *Salmon Single hooks, code M; Salmon Double hooks, code P; or Salmon long shank treble hooks, code X2B*
    Used for all types of salmon and sea trout flies.
8   *McHaffie Master hooks, code MM1B and MM2B*
    These are a recent development on which a wide variety of fly types, both wet and dry may be tied. Using such a hook may greatly reduce the range which needs to be kept.

Armed with the above list of hooks the average flytier will be able to tie any fly for any purpose. You will of course try other types as and when they are available to you. From time to time I have used others.

Swedish dry fly hooks, code K3A
Bronze double hooks, code R1A or R2A
Roman Moser barbless hooks, code CS20
Long shank Mayfly hooks, code D5B
Waddington shanks, code V1B, used with code X1BL or X1BR trebles which are also used for tubes

Threads

Fine strong monocord or similar synthetic thread is excellent on sea trout salmon and large trout flies provided that the colour does not appear as an integral part of the dressing. It sits flat on the hook helping to provide very slim bodies if needed and is strong enough to be pulled very tight when dressing a coarse hair wing like bucktail.

Gossamer silk is not really strong enough for salmon flies with hair wings but is far superior to monocord on representative patterns. The colour range of Pearsell's silk is much better than any synthetic thread I have yet used. Also change of colour is important. Silk darkens in colour when waxed and/or wet. Many natural imitations have been developed with that fact in mind. The Greenwell's Glory is the most famous example. So, when a pattern states a specific shade of silk, silk should be used. Monocord does not change to the same extent.

No matter what type of thread is used it must always be well waxed. Never use liquid wax. It can be unbelievably ·messy and even for dubbing far too much wax ends up on the thread. A solid block of white beeswax is really all that's needed. Keep it in a hand or pocket for a few minutes to soften it sufficiently and draw the required length of thread over the surface just once.

For dubbing fur bodies more wax will be needed. Either draw the thread through some softer wax, or, just as good and easier, rub the original block of wax over the tying thread to be dubbed. Simply hold the thread tightly out from the hook after the tail has been fixed and lightly rub the wax to and fro along it.

Never neglect to wax the thread. There are two reasons why: first, waxed thread grips the hook and materials much better; second, it also helps to keep the thread waterproof. Both are important for ease of tying and durability.

Some flytiers varnish the hook instead of using wax but this is more of a curse than liquid wax.

Tools

A vice of some kind is essential as stated earlier. There are of course many types. A vice of middle price range is what to aim for. There is no need to go over the top pricewise but, on the other hand, too cheap a vice is likely to have jaws which are too large or soft or both. Lever-action vices are much easier to use than those tightened by a wheel. The latter needs to be lubricated regularly.

Very fine sharp scissors are vital. Poorly trimmed ends are unsightly, so you must be able to trim ends tight to the shank. Nail clippers can be of use for the same reason.

Fingers are perfectly good for winding on the thread but you will certainly find a bobbin holder faster, and it is often more accurate.

Small, long-nosed hackle pliers I find are much preferable to the large ones. But a large heavy pair may come in handy for hanging from a material to stop it unravelling while you deal with something else.

A needle is useful, for picking out fur and applying varnish.

Last among the vital tools is the whip finisher. Choose one with large hooks otherwise the thread springs off them with depressing regularity. The dressing often becomes loose and must be partly re-tied if this happens.

There is a huge variety of other available tools, most of which are dispensable, but there are others which I mention in the text (Figure 2.2).

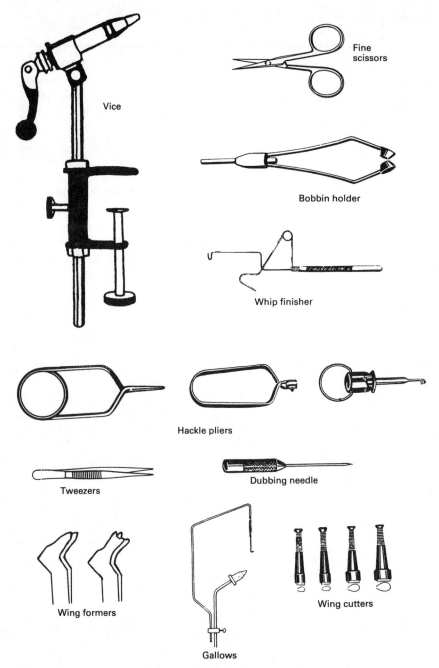

Vice

Fine scissors

Bobbin holder

Whip finisher

Hackle pliers

Tweezers

Dubbing needle

Wing formers

Gallows

Wing cutters

Figure 2.2. There is a wide variety of tools which can be used in constructing flies. Those illustrated here are mentioned throughout this book.

3 Basic Essentials of Flytying

The basic essentials of flytying for *catching fish* are very few and are as follows.

1 Wind the thread evenly, tightly and reasonably neatly around the hook.
2 Use several such turns to bind to the hook small bunches of feather, hair, wool and fur, etc. on top or below the shank. Neatness is not vital but strength is. These turns can also be used for tails, hackles and wings.
3 Wind body materials on to a hook evenly, tightly and neatly. The material should cover everything beneath it and can be of silk, wool tinsel, etc.

    Ribbings can be treated in the same way except that it helps to be able to wind them in the opposite direction to the body material.
4 Wind a hackle over the correct part of the shank evenly, tightly and neatly.
5 For each of 3 and 4 above, secure the material tightly and neatly with several turns of tying thread.
6 Finish the fly with a whip finish or at least several half hitches.

It may seem unusual to begin with such a short summary, but there are valid reasons for it. Hopefully it proves to the sceptic that there is no reason why he or anyone else should not be able to tie flies sufficiently well to gain enjoyment in both the closed and open seasons.

If you are a beginner you can start by using these six points and be selective about which parts of this book to concentrate on first. After you are confident with these you can then branch out and experiment.

If you can wind thread neatly and evenly around a hook you are well on the way to tying good flies. It sounds very easy, but takes time to perfect. The part of the hook where the body will be must be entirely hidden behind close, tight, even turns of well-waxed thread. I usually prefer to begin this as close to the eye of the hook as possible.

Hold the end of the thread in the left hand and bobbin holder in the right. At all times keep the thread pulled tight. Hold the thread diagonally across the nearside of the hook (Figure 3.1). Wind the thread over the hook and away from you so that each turn of the thread is slightly closer to the bend of the hook than the preceding one. This should bind the end held in the left hand firmly to the hook but the turns made with the right hand should never overlap each other. When you have made six or seven turns down the hook the end held by the left hand can be trimmed (Figure 3.2).

On larger hooks, especially those with loop eyes, it is particularly worthwhile to begin as close to the eye as possible. This binds the loop end

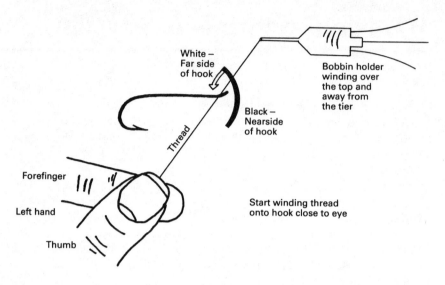

White –
Far side
of hook

Bobbin holder
winding over
the top and
away from
the tier

Black –
Nearside
of hook

Thread

Forefinger

Left hand

Thumb

Start winding thread
onto hook close to eye

Figure 3.1. Winding the tying thread.

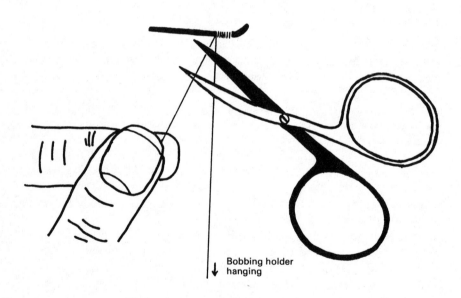

Bobbing holder
hanging

After several turns of thread which secure it to
the hook the thread is held by the left hand
is cut close to the hook

Figure 3.2. Thread secured to hook and trimmed.

tightly to the shank and gives a good flat surface for tying hackles and wings. However, it is a good idea to begin well away from the eye on very small flies. It is all too easy to block the eye with thread, by the time the fly is finished, if you do not leave enough space.

Covering the hook shank with even turns of thread is very important, from the eye of the hook to the bend and back again. After tails, tags and so on are tied in, the close even turns are repeated in the opposite direction. Well-waxed thread gives a good surface for the body material to grip. Partly covered scrap ends of tinsel and feather do not offer this. So, not only the hook should be covered but also all the ends of materials that were tied in at the bend. The result should be a perfectly smooth and tacky base for the body.

Tying thread bodies, such as those of Greenwell's Glory or small Black Pennell, require this level of neatness for there is no covering body material. Why not use it for other flies as well?

This may use a larger amount of thread and be more time consuming than using open turns of thread, but, for durability and smoothness I prefer the method described above.

4 Tags

Salmon fly tags are often composed of two parts: floss silk and tinsel, wire or oval. Trout flies which use tags usually use one or the other but not both.

There are some occasions when I tie in materials under the first winding of thread down the shank — this is one of them.

This may seem like an unusual position to tie in a material which is going to be wound around the hook at the bend. However, it ensures that the tag cannot be pulled loose by the fish's teeth and adds very little bulk to the body.

Basically, there are three methods of attaching any material to the hook. The one you choose depends not only on preference but on the qualities of the material to be tied in.

Method 1

Hold the material by the finger and thumb of each hand so that it is between the vice and the tying thread. The material is lifted around the back of the hook so that the last turn of thread will hold it on whatever part of the hook you require (Figure 4.1). The great advantage of this method is that it is quick and neat and one more turn should secure most materials.

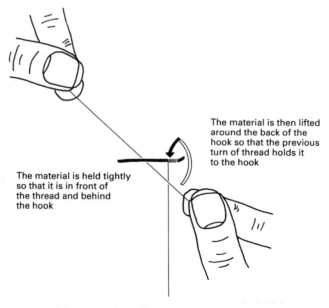

The material is then lifted around the back of the hook so that the previous turn of thread holds it to the hook

The material is held tightly so that it is in front of the thread and behind the hook

Figure 4.1. First method of securing any material of the hook.

Method 2

Hold the material against the required position on the hook and make a few turns of thread around it (Figure 4.2). This is probably the method which beginners try first but it is by no means the easiest. The thread needs to make a loose loop under the shank and, while the thread loop and material are gripped between finger and thumb, the material is fixed by pulling the thread vertically upwards. Another turn or two is usually required after the fingers are removed.

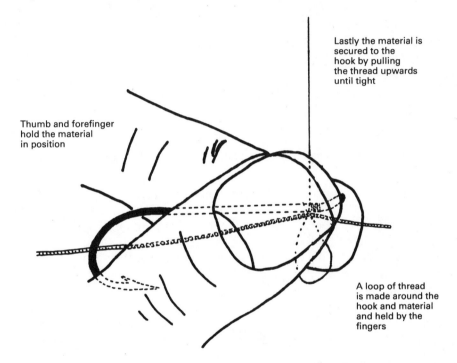

Lastly the material is
secured to the
hook by pulling
the thread upwards
until tight

Thumb and forefinger
hold the material
in position

A loop of thread
is made around the
hook and material
and held by the
fingers

Figure 4.2. Second method of securing any material to the hook – under the shank. If the material is to be tied on top of the shank the loop is made above the hook and the thread is pulled downwards.

Method 3

The third method of tying on material to the hook is to make a loop of floss (for example) around the tying thread and hold it by the left hand (Figure 4.7). Make one turn of thread to hold the floss. Release the floss loop and pull the long end so that a small scrap end remains. One more turn is required to secure the floss.

As the tag material is tied in it should lie along the side of the hook where there is a loop eye (Figure 4.3) or under the shank if you are using a trout hook. When the tag is finished the scrap end should be long enough to reach the end of the eye loop. All other scrap ends of ribbings, body materials, etc. should be the same length. This will help to keep the body smooth.

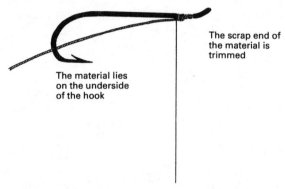

The scrap end of
the material is
trimmed

The material lies
on the underside
of the hook

Figure 4.3. If the hook has a loop eye as with single salmon hooks it is better to tie most materials to the nearside of the hook.

Continue to wind down the hook until the thread hangs in position (Figure 4.4). The thread is immediately returned to the position shown (Figure 4.5) in close even turns (note this is about the width of the barb of the hook). Here it is allowed to hang vertically below the hook while the oval is wound to fill the space (Figure 4.6). The oval is secured at this point with several turns which are continued as before to the position shown (see Figure 4.7).

Figure 4.4. Tag material. Note position of hanging thread on barb.

Figure 4.5. Tag material wound over the top of the hook and away from the tier. Note position of hanging thread on barb.

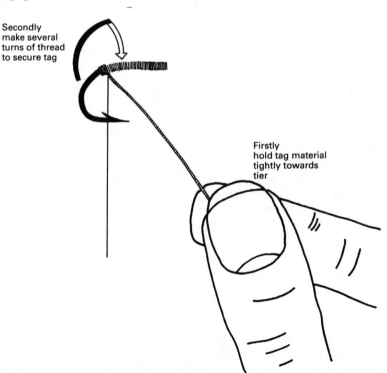

Secondly
make several
turns of thread
to secure tag

Firstly
hold tag material
tightly towards
tier

Figure 4.6. Tag material wound to fill space.

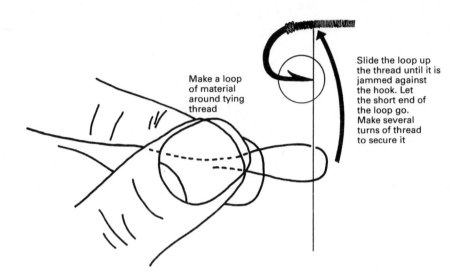

Make a loop
of material
around tying
thread

Slide the loop up
the thread until it is
jammed against
the hook. Let
the short end of
the loop go.
Make several
turns of thread
to secure it

Figure 4.7. Third method of securing any material to the hook. Note position of hanging thread on the hook point.

To secure this, or any other material, to the hook after it has been wound on, the following procedure should be followed. Hold the material horizontally out from the hook — the material should be coming away from the bottom of the hook. Holding the tying thread tightly, make a couple of turns with your other hand. The material should now be secured to the bottom of the hook.

To alter the part of the hook to which the material is secured, simply alter the direction in which the material is held as the securing turns are made; for example, if the material is held vertically up or down it will be secured to the side of the hook.

If you wish, the oval can be trimmed close to the hook at this point, or the scrap end can be left long enough to reach the tying postion (see Figure 4.1). The latter method means that the tag can never be pulled out of place and adds virtually no bulk to the body.

The thread is then wound evenly to the right until it can hang vertically downwards at the hook point (see Figure 4.7). Take a length of floss silk and tie it on with several turns of thread at this point.

Marabou floss is by far the best type to use. Minute threads do not break away from it in all directions, a problem with many of the synthetic flosses, and it has a lustre which is unmatched. For all uses I prefer to untwist it and use one of its two strands. This does not mean that a spool lasts longer because a double layer is wound on to the hook. The advantage in splitting it is that the fibres lie flatter so it is easy to obtain a very smooth finish.

Wind the floss evenly down to meet the oval and back again to where the tying thread is hanging, where several turns will fix it in place. Trim off the end in the same way as the oval part of the tag (Figure 4.8).

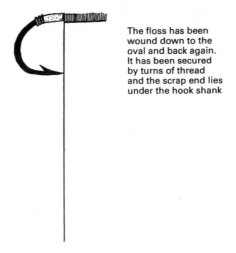

The floss has been wound down to the oval and back again. It has been secured by turns of thread and the scrap end lies under the hook shank

Figure 4.8 Finished tag.

Double and treble hooks often do not have the floss element of the tag. If they do the procedure is as before. However, the oval or wire portion is tied differently. It is fixed to the hook as before close to the eye, but this time it is whipped to the shank only as far as the hanging thread (see Figure 4.7). As the thread is allowed to hang, the oval is wound on towards the bend for three or four turns. It is then brought between the bends of the hooks and pulled firmly towards the eye of the hook. It is held in this position while several turns of thread secure it (Figure 4.9). In this way there is no chance of the tag slipping back.

What possible function does a tag serve? On some natural representations it may signify a hatching insect leaving its shuck behind, a bunch of eggs on a female adult or even an air bubble. Here it may justifiably claim to be an important part of the deception.

On non-representative patterns things are very different. The average salmon fly represents nothing at all. I have read somewhere that it optically separates the hook from the fly, so that the fish's attention is directed towards the dressing rather than the hook dangling beneath it. I find this hard to believe. There is no doubt in my mind that, although it is the first part of the fly to be tied, a tag is simply there to add a little extra to the dressing as a finishing touch.

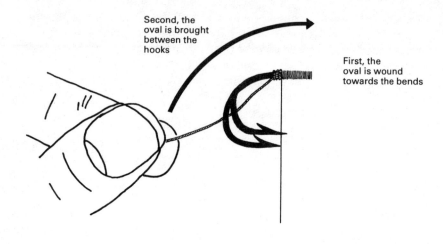

Second, the
oval is brought
between the
hooks

First, the
oval is wound
towards the bends

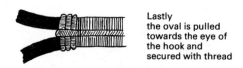

Lastly
the oval is pulled
towards the eye of
the hook and
secured with thread

Figure 4.9. Tag on a double hook. Note position of hanging thread on hook point.

5 Tails

Much here depends on the kind of tail which is required, particularly with a view to its length. (See Part Two, 'Proportions'.)

The tail material, whatever it is, is secured at the bend of the hook by a few turns of thread. Regardless of the amount required to be visible, I leave a long scrap end in the same way as the oval tinsel used for the tag. This has two functions, for as well as giving strength, it removes the chance of an unsightly lump appearing at the tail end of the body. Usually, if a fly's body is to be tapered, it should be done with the thinnest end, at the tail. Thoughtless over-trimming reverses this. An aesthetic point rather than vital for practical reasons. Most tail materials are slim enough not to add bulk to the body. Wool can be an exception. I don't often like fly tails to look too bulky so the problem is solved by splitting the wool in the same fashion as the floss silk mentioned earlier.

I am a firm advocate of tails being as short as is practical no matter what material is used. In most cases the less material straggling behind the bend of the hook the better. Like so many other aspects of flytying and fishing, this statement must be qualified. Tail length depends on its purpose. To be representative a dun or spinner tail will be long in comparison with the body, a nymph's tail will usually be much shorter. Also the shape of the hook may be important, as the distance between the tie-in point and a vertical line drawn through the rear of the bend will vary greatly. On traditional style wet flies tail length is more a matter of personal choice than anything else.

It is too simple to say that all tails are fixed at the bend. Certain variations may be useful: for example, tying the tail of a dun a little further round the bend will point it downwards, offering a little extra support for keeping the fly afloat; a midge pupa's 'breather' will be well round the bend to give a realistic shape; on a low-water salmon pattern the tail will be tied in only one half to two-thirds of the way down the shank.

Other than wool, tails can be made from a variety of materials. The most common is cock or hen hackle fibre, particularly for ephemeroptera or up-winged patterns (Plate 8). Simply pull a small bunch of fibres from the stalk, hold them between finger and thumb of the left hand so that the desired amount of fibre extends behind the tie-in point. Bring the thread vertically upwards between the thumb and the hook. Slip the thread between the forefinger and the hook leaving a small loop of thread above the fingers. Draw the thread vertically downwards (the opposite of Figure 4.2). Several more turns may be needed to hold the tail fast.

The number of fibres used for such a tail can vary. Use only two or three if what you want is a 'copy' of the natural. However, it is unnecessary to be that fussy. A few extra fibres will not detract from the appearance but will enhance its ability to float.

The best feathers to use for tails are those found at the sides of a cock cape, the feathers are short and broad and the fibres are long and stiff.

Many of the traditional wet fly patterns call for ibis substitute tails. The best way to make these, and tails made from feather fibre of similar texture, is to cut a section of six to eight fibres from the feather. Fold the fibres over, this helps keep the tail from sticking out at the wrong angle. Tie in the tail as before, holding the tail so that as the thread is pulled tight the fibres are pressed down on top of each other. This method can also be used for making simple folded or rolled wings.

Golden pheasant crest tails are tied in by this method and usually exceed the bend of the hook. For myself, I find their natural upward pointing curve makes this acceptable (see Figure 4.1). This method is also useful for fixing other parts of the dressing, such as body materials or hackles. It is not suitable for most wings, however, but there is one advantage in this method, especially on small flies, in that it reduces the number of turns required to hold the material.

When a fly is fished very slowly in stillwater or upstream in a river the hackle tends to sit out from the hook and may represent a drowned dun or spinner. When fished more quickly or downstream the hackle fibres are drawn back over the body so that the fly takes on the profile of a swimming nymph. The hackle fibres ought to be soft, just long enough to imply the presence of a tail when the fibres are drawn back.

Conversely many non-representative patterns, such as the Grouse and Claret, have their designs based on representative flies. Often the only differences between these two types is size and gaudiness. Nevertheless, they retain tails whose practical purpose is questionable.

The purpose of a representative pattern is to deceive the fish into thinking the fly is edible. A non-representative fly is supposed to arouse the fish's memory of feeding or some other basic impulse. There is no logical reason why these two types of fly, for totally different purposes, should have similar construction or appearance. Why, then, is it all too common to have these flies tied in the same way? Habit, not knowing any better and the fact that they do catch fish are all part of the answer. Think beforehand whether or not a tail is really required. Sea trout flies, such as the Medicine, seem to work perfectly well without (Plate 13).

6 Butts

These tend to be of ostrich herl or wool, most often black or red. They occur only rarely on trout flies and are restricted primarily to the traditional dressings of salmon flies.

Whether or not a butt plays an important part in a fish's 'thinking' before taking or rejecting a fly I very much doubt. Butts are pleasing to the eye though, and more important can help to hide small imperfections in the dressing of tag and tails.

After the tail has been secured, the silk is brought up the shank from the point where that tail has been fixed, in close even turns. This distance varies with hook size but is generally between 1 mm and 3 mm (Figure 6.1).

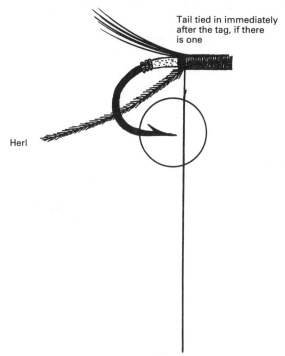

Tail tied in immediately after the tag, if there is one

Herl

Figure 6.1. Tying the butt. Note position of hanging thread.

At this point the herl is tied in the same way as the golden pheasant crest (see Figure 4.1). I like to bring the herl over the top of the hook and secure it on the side of the shank facing me. Leave long scrap ends as before.

The herl must be tied in the right way for appearance and ease of tying. Hold the herl horizontally and look at it. The stalk should be visible at the top as a straight edge and the fibres should point downwards from it.

Make one turn of the herl back down the hook to the tail. By that time you will be able to see in what direction the fibres of the herl will point. If they do not point towards the tail, tie in the herl again. Wind the herl around the hook in close even turns back to where the thread is hanging and secure it in the usual way. The turns of thread and herl are always laid on the hook side by side, they must never overlap each other (Figure 6.2).

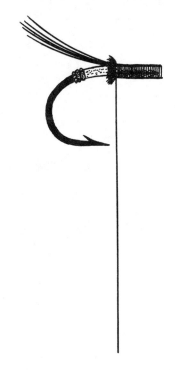

Figure 6.2. Finished butt. Fibres of herl point towards the hook bend. The scrap ends of all the materials tied in so far lie along the hook shank to be covered by the body.

If wool is used as a butt, two or three turns ought to be enough. I tie the wool in at the tail, wind the thread a little towards the eye and follow it immediately with the wool. Shaggy wool produces the best results.

Butts can also look well if fur is dubbed onto the tying thread as it hangs after tying the tail. The thread is then wound for two or three turns towards the eye. (See 'Bodies'.)

7 Ribbings

There are basically three functions which a rib may have on any fly: strength, attraction and/or realism.

A well-tied rib ought to add strength to the body especially when it is composed of delicate materials such as fur or mylar tinsel. The rib should prevent premature or total loss of body material. This capacity is greatly enhanced by the rib being wound in the opposite direction to the body material. Should a break occur there will only be partial unravelling.

A rib is a useful item for strengthening a body hackle as well. There are two ways to achieve this. First, the hackle can be wound over the body first (see 'Bodies'). The ribbing material which must be fine thread or wire, is then wound through the hackle. Second, the rib can be wound onto the body before the hackle. The hackle is then wound beside the rear edge of the rib, and very close to it. The hackle stalk is then protected by the rib from the fish's teeth. This method is one which I prefer. It is most successful on larger flies when the rib may be of medium to large oval. The first method is more a feature of trout rather than salmon flies (Figure 7.1).

Whichever form is used, the ribbing turns must be evenly spread. If it is not the rib is prone to slipping towards the tail. Strength is, to my mind, the most important function on almost every fly. Attraction is entirely determined by the materials used for both the body and the rib.

On a floss silk body any rib will rest on top of the body and be easily visible but on a fur body it really depends on how bushy the fur is. A rib may be hardly noticeable when it is tied, particularly if the fur is further picked out with a needle (Figure 7.2).

Tinsel of varying types is most commonly used as ribbing. The sparkle which this creates is naturally thought to be a contributory factor in the attractiveness of many flies. There is a school of thought that suggests use of tinsel (or other very bright materials such as fluorescent floss) may be counterproductive in some circumstances. By using a complementary shade of tying thread to rib representative flies, a more realistic impression of a segmented body may result. Less reflective materials than tinsel such as herl, silk and so on may well produce a more realistic look on some flies. Roger Fogg in *The Art of the Wet Fly* (1979) certainly advocates this on his spider wet flies, but what exactly do we mean by a realistic fly?

Many flytiers aim to caricature natural insects rather than to copy them. The idea is simply to pick out certain features which are thought to be important and exaggerate them. One example of this is the broad silver tinsel rib, or tag, on a Corixa which may well be a caricature of the air bubble the creature carries with it under water (Plate 5).

We are also led here into the more difficult question of what looks

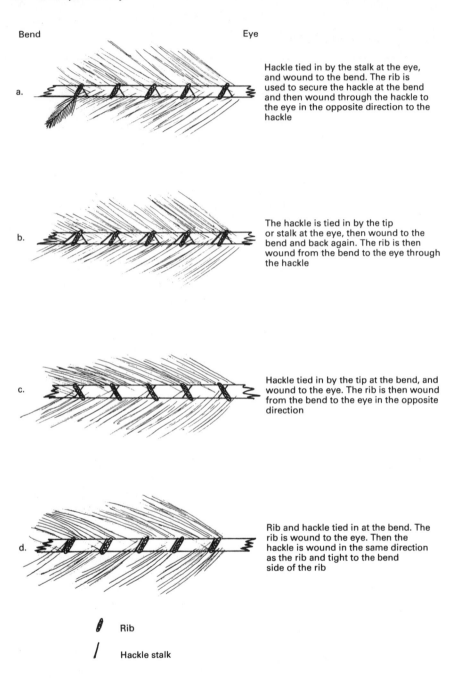

Bend   Eye

a.   Hackle tied in by the stalk at the eye, and wound to the bend. The rib is used to secure the hackle at the bend and then wound through the hackle to the eye in the opposite direction to the hackle

b.   The hackle is tied in by the tip or stalk at the eye, then wound to the bend and back again. The rib is then wound from the bend to the eye through the hackle

c.   Hackle tied in by the tip at the bend, and wound to the eye. The rib is then wound from the bend to the eye in the opposite direction

d.   Rib and hackle tied in at the bend. The rib is wound to the eye. Then the hackle is wound in the same direction as the rib and tight to the bend side of the rib

Rib

Hackle stalk

Figure 7.1. Various methods of tying a rib and body or palmered hackles.

realistic to us may not do so to a fish. Reflection, refraction, surface ripple, the mirror image of the bottom on the underside of the surface, distortion due to the angle of the fish's vision in relation to its window, movement of the current carrying plenty of debris and light intensity: some or all of these combine to make the fish's view of a fly potentially very different to our own. This is true of all parts of the artificial fly, and it raises more questions than it answers.

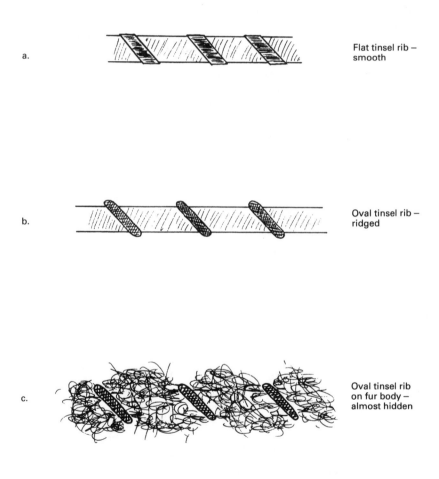

a. Flat tinsel rib – smooth

b. Oval tinsel rib – ridged

c. Oval tinsel rib on fur body – almost hidden

Figure 7.2. A tied rib incorporating various materials.

Midge pupae patterns may well use polythene as a rib over feather fibre or fur bodies. Occasionally it may cover the whole body. Polythene combines reflectiveness with translucency which makes a very realistic body when viewed in air. When viewed by a fish in water, can we be sure? Nylon fishing line dyed or clear has similar qualities and possibly more applications than polythene.

Generally speaking, all materials to be tied onto the hook should be whipped on top of the thread which was wound on the shank at the beginning. There are several exceptions, notably the rib and dry fly wings.

I prefer on most flies, particularly those without tags, to tie in the rib as soon as the thread is secured on the hook (see Figures 4.1 and 4.2). The thread is continued down the shank to the bend where the tail is fixed. The shank is covered with another even layer of tying thread and the body material, making sure that enough space is left near the eye for hackles and wings before the rib is wound on top.

I use the above procedure on trout flies. It is not possible to do this on salmon flies on which the tag, tail and butt must be finished before the rib is attached. I find it useful always to tie and finish the rib underneath the hook on ordinary eyed hooks. It is important that it should be finished in this manner to avoid any lumps under the point where the wings are tied on. This ploy removes the possibility of the wing set being altered by roughness which may be present at this point.

Four, five or six turns of rib along the body are usually ample. This may vary slightly depending on the body length and thickness of the rib. A long-shank Mayfly is one of the very few occasions when I use more turns. A small number of turns is enough to imply a segmented body on most naturals regardless of how many segments the real thing may have.

There are other ways to add a rib which fulfils the required functions. With herl bodies for example I find it useful to twist a length of wire around several herls. The whole body and rib are wound on simultaneously. This may result in a slightly more scruffy body than other methods but it is very durable. Black and Peacock Spiders and Worm Flies are made in this way (Plate 4).

There is an exception to tying in the rib beneath the hook. As with the oval part of a tag on salmon flies tied on hooks with loop eyes, the rib is fixed to the side of the hook on which the loop of the eye tapers onto the shank. This is extremely useful on such hooks where the end of the loop does not end in a point as it ought to, because it helps to even out a lump which would otherwise be visible through the body.

One final idea worth trying only when a rib is wound over a tinsel body, is to cover the finished body and rib with a few drops of superglue or varnish. The result is very durable and the rib never slips. Be careful to let the glue dry well before adding the remainder of the dressing.

8 Underbodies

There are four main reasons for putting an underbody on a fly: to complement the colour and shade of the body through a translucent body material (such as seal's fur); to produce the required body shape; to enable the fly to sink deep quickly by adding weight; and to add flotation with a buoyant material.

Except for my SB patterns I seldom feel the need to use an underbody, because thoughtful choice of hooks and materials can often produce the desired effect by themselves.

There are two reasons for avoiding underbodies: first, bulk is added to the body — an advantage on some flies like sedge pupae, but unwanted in many others; second, it means extra work at the vice.

When colour is the only consideration the correct choice of tying thread used is important. If this thread is to show through the fur it is important that the correct steps are taken (see 'Basic Essentials of Flytying'). This is another reason for covering as much of the ribbing as possible, before winding on the body.

To add bulk to a sedge pupa body no underbody is needed — simply dub a great deal of fur onto the thread and apply it correctly (see 'Bodies'). This is simple and quick to dress but is not very satisfactory as any ribbing will disappear into the fur when wound on. Also the fur is too easily pulled by fish teeth so the profile of the body is soon lost. This, of course, does not mean it will catch fewer fish. An alternative, and better, way is to build up several layers of floss silk to form the correct shape. Over this is wound lightly dubbed fur and a rib wound in the opposite direction. This way the profile will be maintained, there will still be an impression of translucency, and durability will be increased.

A very useful technique which is excellent in terms of translucency is to use tinsel underbody wrapped over with very lightly dubbed fur. The use of lurex or Lureflash greatly extends the colour range. If the dubbing is too heavy the value of the underbody is lost (Plates 2 and 3).

To add weight is a frequent reason for using an underbody. This can be partly achieved by the choice of an appropriate hook gauge. Often this is not enough. Usually the copper or lead foil or wire has a shaping function or may help the fly to 'swim' upside down, as well as sinking it quickly. Lead is the better of the two in terms of its weight-volume ratio.

Regardless of the material, if it is wound around the length of the shank weight is its only purpose. But if foil wire or shot is fixed to one end of the hook, the manner in which the fly sinks and fishes will be quite different from an evenly or unweighted fly. A Dog Nobbler, not very appealing in name or appearance, is weighted only near the eye. Thus it dives rapidly

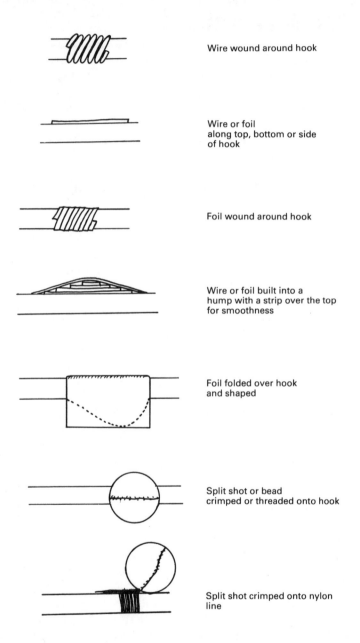

Wire wound around hook

Wire or foil
along top, bottom or side
of hook

Foil wound around hook

Wire or foil built into a
hump with a strip over the top
for smoothness

Foil folded over hook
and shaped

Split shot or bead
crimped or threaded onto hook

Split shot crimped onto nylon
line

All may be glued and/or bound with thread

Figure 8.1. Weighting the hook.

head first and is raised by each pull on the line. The combination of pattern and motion can be deadly particularly when used for rainbow trout in stillwater (Figure 8.1 and Plate 2).

Fixing weight only to the top of the shank makes the hook sink upside down. This may be a distinct advantage when fishing over weeds or rocks. It obviously helps to prevent snagging but it is not foolproof. This technique can be employed successfully in both lures and representations of nymphs and larvae. Stick flies and Mayfly nymphs (Plate 9) are the most familiar examples.

Weight under the body can also help to add realism. The shape of a freshwater shrimp is often gained in this way. Here, successively shorter strips of foil or wire are bound to the top of the hook. This helps to produce the characteristic arched back of the real thing.

Another fly/lure which may use a lead underbody both for weight and shape is the Zonker. This is designed to represent a small fish. A piece of lead foil is folded over the top of the hook and shaped below with nail clippers into a semi-circle. This is superglued and pressed into position with pliers. When covered with an overbody of mylar piping the impression of a fish is very realistic. My view is that this bulging body below the shank effectively closes the gape of the hook, a problem which might be overcome by tying these lures upside-down.

Wire, if it is fine enough, can also be used instead of tying thread becoming not just an underbody but an integral part of the whole construction. (Incidentally, a cheap way of obtaining very fine copper wire is to strip the plastic coating from a piece of electrical cable.) Sawyer's Pheasant Tail nymph exemplifies the method (Plate 5). To avoid the problem of the wire slipping over the hook, simply wax it in exactly the same fashion as tying thread.

In all flies, weighted or otherwise, a solid foundation is vital. The more underbody material which is required the greater the tendency for it to slip around the shank. If the foundation moves the top dressing will follow naturally. Very tight turns of strong fine thread ought to suffice but a few drops of varnish or superglue will add extra insurance. Superglue is the better choice in my opinion.

Flotation, as with weight, is helped by choosing the correct hooks — in this case the finest wire possible. Non-absorbent materials and fine quality stiff hackles have traditionally been used for dry flies. Increasing the surface area of the fly to reduce the pressure on the water surface also helps flotation, as with dapping flies.

Underbody flotation is useful for two possible reasons: first, to keep the fly on the surface; and second, and less common, to reduce the rate of sinking.

Cork, plastozote, deer hair, to name but a few, can be wrapped around the shank, tied in strips along it or glued on in shaped lumps. Snails, corixa or bushy dry flies are all possible hosts for such underbodies though I have found these of little practical use for my own fishing. All three of these materials are also usable in floating fly patterns and surface lures for sea trout, for example the Razzler.

9 Bodies

What exactly is the purpose of an artificial fly's body? On the face of it an obvious question which requires no answer. But this is not so. If we simply say that the fly's body should resemble the body of a natural fly, we ignore a large range of possibilities. Anglers can speculate unendingly about the degree to which any part of an artificial fly mimics a natural with very little chance of being 100 per cent confident that they are right. If we design a fly body, or any other part for that matter, to suit a particular set of conditions and it works, how can we be sure that the fish took it for the 'right' reason? This is what makes our sport so fascinating.

The body may indeed be constructed to represent a natural. But to whose eye, our own or that of the fish? Few artificial flies are anything better than simple cartoons of the real thing. Translucency or reflectiveness may be the main qualities of the body, with accidental or intentional resemblance to the natural, but the body may be a fancy attractive feature in itself. These are only a few of the possibilities and any one fly may combine several. An artificial fly's body is very rarely intended to be seen in isolation. The combination of hackles, wings, tails and so on may modify its appearance in or out of the water. An excellent example of such a combination is the Medicine fly (Plate 13). The body is very slim and made of reflective tinsel set between highly translucent, mobile and lightly dressed hackle and hair wing. The overall impression is what is important, not each part individually.

On the other hand the body of a representative insect pattern may be of more importance on its own — after all that is where the meat is.

My purpose here is *not* to give reliable answers. I doubt if there are any. I hope simply to encourage thought and experiment and a little critical analysis of why a fly regularly succeeds or fails.

Tying thread

Bodies tied with thread are the slimmest possible bodies, without painting the hook or leaving it undressed. They require perfect neatness in winding the thread both ways along the hook. Some opinion recommends these as the simplest for beginners but I do not agree. One careless turn leaving a gap for tail stubs to show through, or a turn which overlaps others can so easily spoil the appearance. However, with experience, this close even type of thread body becomes easy and quick to tie. A bobbin holder is invaluable for this, helping increase both speed and control and it is much more effective than using one's fingers.

There are a number of materials that can be used to tie bodies. Surely the best types to start with are those which are not only simple but also hide imperfections. For me wool is the perfect choice.

Wool

Embroidery wool is my favourite type. It has the advantage of cheapness and is available in a wide range of shades. Darning wools are also good, partly because they are finer and because they tend to have blended shades which produce more subtle bodies than single shade wools.

The embroidery wool I use has four strands though for all flies this is at least reduced to two and for small flies or where a smoother body is needed one strand is best. The single strand on its own is very weak so it must be treated with more delicacy.

Simply tie in under the shank after the tail, if any, has been fixed. Use any of the three methods described earlier (see 'Tags'). Leave enough of a scrap end that can be whipped all along the shank adding strength and smoothness to the body. (This is the same procedure for nearly all body materials.) After the tying thread is wound back towards the eye, leaving enough room for hackles and wings, wind on the wool in close even turns to the same position where it is tied in under the hook by several turns of thread and trimmed off close (Figure 9.1).

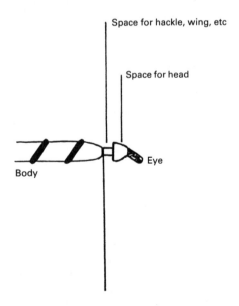

Figure 9.1. Leaving space for wings, hackles and head.

Wool is a fine enough material for use in the smallest flies, with a few stray fibres adding to its translucency. It can be a serviceable substitute for either floss or seal's fur on many patterns. Picking at the finished body with a needle or attacking it with sandpaper helps to improve the effect of the seal's fur.

In my opinion, wool has been a very under-used material, perhaps because it does not sound as exotic as seal. I prefer it to either floss silk or fur for the bodies of many of my sea trout and salmon flies, particularly for shrimps (Plates 15 and 16).

The following materials are applied in a similar manner to that of wool.

Chenille

Choice of good quality materials is often the key to successful fly dressing. This is certainly true of chenille. Poor varieties have a frustrating habit of loosing their 'fluff' during application. Hold the length of chenille with hackle pliers, rather than the fingers, when winding it onto the hook, disintegration is thus minimised.

The only difference to tying wool is that a little of the fluff must be removed leaving only the core to be tied in, otherwise the body may become ridiculously fat. A little fluff may also be scraped away after the chenille has been wound so that, again, the material is fixed to the hook by the core.

The use of chenille is almost totally confined to gaudy stillwater rainbow trout lures. To this end fluorescent and sparkling chenille are also available in a variety of gauges. I don't like over-bright flies, though they have a place in the angler's armoury. Lures do not have to be like that. The Ace of Spades uses chenille, it is both sombre and elegant.

Herl

If a very neat body is required, a single peacock or ostrich herl of good quality may be used. The problem here is that unless the body is well ribbed it will not be very durable. However, there are other options to answer this problem, depending on the degree of neatness, bulk and strength required. First, several herls may be twisted together and tied in as normal — strong but seldom neat. Second, twist several herls together with a length of wire which increases strength (Plate 4). Third, use a single herl and varnish the shank before it is wound on, which should be much neater (Figure 9.2).

Choose whichever method suits the effect which you want to create. But if the last is your choice be very careful. If too much varnish is used it will

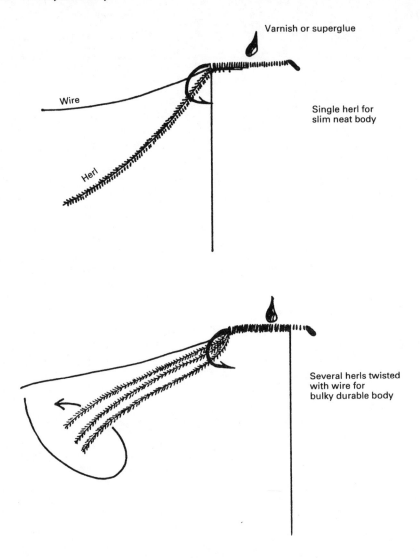

Varnish or superglue

Wire

Herl

Single herl for
slim neat body

Several herls twisted
with wire for
bulky durable body

Figure 9.2. Using a single herl and several herls.

soak through the herl leaving the fibres stiff and lifeless. The herl cannot be partly unwound if you are unhappy with its appearance.

If only one herl is to be used, consider in what direction the fibres of the herl should point. If they point in the wrong direction the herl is upside-down. Untie it, turn it around and start again. It is conventional for the fibres to point tailwards (see 'Butts').

A long-fibred herl, such as ostrich, can form a very attractive body if it is wound in the normal way using a single herl. When it is secure, and before the rib is wound, the herl fibres may be trimmed with a pair of fine sharp scissors all around the hook and close to it.

Stripped herl

Many of the flies making use of stripped herl have the word quill in their names: Orange Quill, Ginger Quill and so on. They are largely out of favour with modern flytiers, because they are solid and lifeless when seen in silhouette against the light. They also reflect light rather than being translucent. Since a fish often views the fly against the sky, quills have been relegated in favour of more translucent furs, feather, fibres, etc. Nonetheless, they still account for their fair share of fish when they are used.

Ribbing a quill body instantly destroys the segmented appearance, but something is needed to improve their poor lifespan. The answer is to add a little clear varnish below or on top of the body or both.

To strip the herl of its fibres, hold it by the tip and grip it between the forefinger tip and thumbnail of the other hand near to the tip. Draw these fingers along the herl so that the thumbnail scrapes the fibres from one side of the herl. Repeat this several times for each side of the herl. The thumbnail must be placed on the herl firmly but gently (Figure 9.3). The

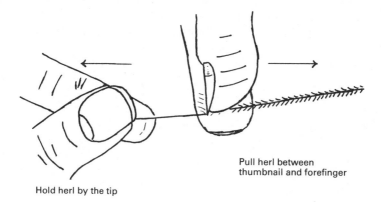

Pull herl between
thumbnail and forefinger

Hold herl by the tip

Figure 9.3. Stripping the herl.

fibres may also be removed by scraping with a razor blade or a rubber but I prefer using my thumbnail.

Peacock herls are usually the only ones to be scraped in this way, and their scope will be enlarged by dyeing. It is also worth noting that herls taken from near the eye of the feather have better markings and are generally of better quality than those near the base. The main problem with peacock herls is their brittleness so care must be taken to avoid frustrating breaks.

Feather fibre

Most wing and tail feathers, either natural or dyed, can be used provided they have long fine fibres such as found in pheasant tail, heron and condor. Substitutes of the last two are traditionally the most common. Three to four fibres are usually sufficient, twisted or otherwise, to form the bodies of small and representative patterns (Plates 6 and 8). There are few other types of fly which have such a body. Durability is less of a problem than it is with herls, but can be improved in the same ways if required.

Stripped Hackle Stacks

These are also used for representative flies, in particular spinners such as Lunn's Particular and Houghton's Ruby. A hackle stalk has the same lifeless problem as stripped herl. However, it does have the advantage of producing a neat tapered body, the stalk being naturally tapered, without any need for extra turns of thread to build up an underbody. It will also imply a segmented body.

Strip the fibres from a cock hackle of the required colour. If a dyed stalk is to be used it may be a good idea to dye the stalk after it has been stripped. Thus an even colour can be obtained all round the stalk. When a hackle is dyed before the fibres are removed, two white lines will show clearly where the fibres use to be.

Such bodies are tied in exactly as wool or quill but their limited use means they are only of minor importance.

Tinsel

There are several varieties. These range from the old stiff metal to the newer softer mylar type. I think that the first type can be disregarded. It is difficult to get even gapless turns and the wider tinsels are difficult to fix to the hook neatly, at least for beginners. Because metal tinsel is so rigid the tying thread can be cut easily and the finished body is prone to tarnishing.

Mylar is quite the reverse. It is soft enough to tie in neatly no matter how wide and turns can be made side-by-side or partially overlapping to give a slightly ridged effect. Mylar will not tarnish and has the added advantage that it may be silver on one side and gold on the other, obviously reducing the number of spools to be bought. When using dual-coloured tinsel the body colour which is desired must be placed against the hook with the unwanted colour outwards. When the tinsel is wound on the required colour will appear on top (Figure 9.4).

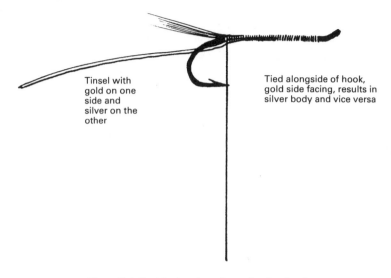

Tinsel with gold on one side and silver on the other

Tied alongside of hook, gold side facing, results in silver body and vice versa

Figure 9.4. Positioning the colour of mylar tinsel.

There are two points to bear in mind with mylar. First, it is likely to be marked or torn if exposed regularly to fish teeth. A top coat of varnish or superglue solves this. Such a ploy is helpful when the tinsel overlaps itself and will also prevent slippage of wire or oval ribs. The result is a solid and very secure body which can take a lot of punishment. Mylar is also much lighter than the old metal tinsels, a distinct advantage in tying several dry flies, for example the Wickham's Fancy. On wet flies a slightly heavier hook can be used to compensate for the reduction in weight when mylar is used.

The second point is that much less skill is required to make a good job with soft tinsel. Whether or not you consider this a good thing is entirely a matter of opinion. It may be a pity not to be able to use the more skilful material but it is of no interest to the fish.

If there is no tag or butt, tinsel can be tied in at the same position as the ribbing, near the eye (see Figure 4.9) or it may be tied in after the tail. Strips of the required width can be cut from a sheet of mylar (or a crisp packet to do the same job). There may be an advantage in being able to make small adjustments to the width but this is negligible. If a less than razor-sharp knife is used the edge will be rough and unsightly. All in all, foil-type sheets are more bother than they are worth for average needs.

Lurex and Lureflash products are alternatives to tinsel which dramatically increase the range of colours which are available. Lurex is very similar to mylar tinsel in texture, but is very narrow and gives a wide range of shades. Some products, though, have a nasty habit of the colour 'washing' off. Adding varnish or glue only serves to make this happen while the hook is still in the vice. My solution is to cover a lurex body with a layer of very fine polythene, cut into a strip and wound over the lurex as if it were tinsel. Thin polythene is useful to ensure none of the colour of the lurex is lost. A blue lurex body tied in this way over two-thirds of the shank with a black cock hackle makes a superb Bluebottle spider.

The wide range of shades can be used to make interesting combinations of lurex, tinsel or Lureflash underbody and lightly dubbed seal fur overbody which can complement or contrast with each other in an effort to improve the translucent qualities of the body (Plates 2 and 3).

Oval

Oval is normally a ribbing material, but it can be used to produce a more textured tinsel body. Embossed tinsel will do much the same job with rather less bulk. Used in exactly the same way as the preceding body materials, oval is most often seen on salmon flies such as shrimps. It can produce a pleasing effect if a fat shiny textured body is needed, but it is difficult to avoid small gaps at the beginning and end of the winding. This is most difficult to disguise with broad oval. Despite its bulk it is very important to have a very smooth underbody in order to avoid unevenness or gaps appearing between the turns.

Oval bodies can be more pleasing to the eye than flat tinsel because their reflective qualities are not as harsh as ordinary tinsel. This idea is used to good effect on the Delphi.

Mylar piping

I seldom use piping as it is almost exclusively a rainbow trout lure material, a style in which I have little interest. It can also be used for tube flies which I generally leave undressed (Plate 14). On most flies where it is used I feel sure that a normal tinsel body would suffice. The only advantage it has is that tinsel bodies of considerable depth or steep taper are possible when normal winding of tinsel would be impossible, such as Zonkers.

A suitable length is cut and the core cord very gently removed, leaving a mesh of tinsel tubing which is slipped over the eye of the hook and along the shank. Two separate tyings are needed, one at each end of the body. Each is finished off and varnished.

The worst problem to be faced is the delicacy of pipings. All too easily the woven tinsel will unravel. Additionally, there are the difficulties of keeping the mesh tight enough to reduce the opportunity for fish teeth to pull at it, plus the possibility of unsightly gaps appearing in the mesh. All this means that I do not enjoy using it so I seldom do. Other people find it much more appealing. However, it is possible to produce a tinsel tail by leaving a length of piping behind the bend and unravelling it after it has been securely tied to the hook (Figure 9.5.).

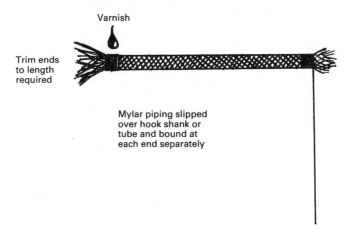

Figure 9.5. Mylar piping body.

One other problem which makes piping more time consuming to tie is that an underbody of floss is needed. When this is finished the thread must be tied off and secured with varnish. Then, when the piping is slipped on it to be secured separately front and rear, it leaves two whippings to be varnished.

Floss silk

As with the tag, Marabou floss is the best type unless fluorescent floss is needed. It is applied in the same double layer fashion as with the tag. One point worth considering especially with representative patterns is that silk darkens slightly when wet. Just like all other aspects of fly construction, always think how it will look when in use, not how it looks in the vice. The degree of floss colour change will vary greatly between materials — silk or synthetic and different makes.

If a tapered body is needed, no underbody is required. Simply tie in the floss at the head and wrap it down the hook but not quite as far as the tail and back towards the eye. This is repeated several times, each time taking the floss less far down the shank. Finally wrap the floss all the way to the tail and back again. Any degree of taper may be obtained in this way. Finish the floss under the shank in the normal way (Figure 9.6).

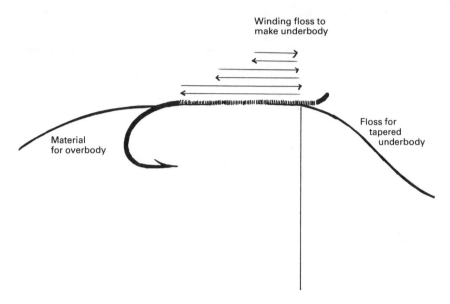

Figure 9.6. Obtaining a degree of taper.

Using floss silk makes a slightly fatter body than that of plain tying thread. There is one other difference. Tying thread should be waxed whereas floss is not. The shade of tying thread will be darkened when waxed and then wound tightly on the hook. The Greenwell's Glory made with waxed primrose silk is matched almost perfectly by an olive floss silk body.

There are a few exceptions to the tying of level, or evenly tapered, bodies as described above. Ants or any other flies which require lumpy bodies will utilise marginally different methods. Simply wind the floss six or seven times over the spot near the tail, make one layer over the middle of the body and repeat the lump at the top of the body. It sounds very easy, but it does not always work perfectly. The turns of floss may, sooner or later, slip over each other so that lumps become loose. A turn or two of wool or dubbed fur might be more successful.

Fur

Regardless of what fur is used, the technique for tying is nearly always the same. However, some furs are easier to dub than others. The method I prefer has the virtues of speed and simplicity. First, the correct tying silk must be chosen, before the fly is begun. This may be of two types: exactly the same shade as the thread, so that this plays as little part as possible in the appearance of the finished fly; or, alternatively, a complementary or contrasting thread may be visible through the finished dubbing to become an integral part of the body colour.

The fur is then chosen and prepared. This is a little more involved than may at first appear — decisions must be made on the shade, or shades, required and how slim or shaggy the final body must be. For example, if a pattern calls for hare's ear without any other details given, we may have a problem. A hare's ear includes fur of widely differing length and shades varying from light tan to black. To solve this we need to have a very clear idea of the effect we wish to create for the whole body or any part of it.

There is no substitute for experience of what works and what looks right. The following general rules may be useful, but as ever there are plenty of exceptions.

No matter which fur is used, take a piece which you think will be a suitable amount. Put half of it back in the packet and you will probably still have more than enough. It is always easier to add more dubbing than to remove it.

There is usually no need to use a separate thread for dubbing the fur onto, unless you wish to use a floss underbody to make a bulky body which is not too shaggy. The G & H Sedge is another exception. At the tail end of such a fly two lengths of well-waxed silk are tied in. After the deer hair has been spun on and trimmed to shape (Figure 9.9) the fur is dubbed onto each length of silk in turn. These are then twisted together before being drawn along the underside of the body and secured near the head (Figure 9.7).

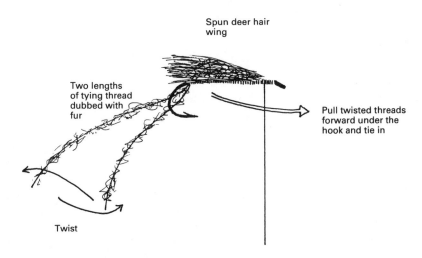

Figure 9.7. The body of the G & H sedge.

The fur is dubbed directly onto the tying thread which should have a little extra wax rubbed on to it. Usually fur bodies are slightly tapered which requires a very small amount of dubbing at the tail and progressively more nearer the head. Alternatively, a light dubbing can be used throughout so it must be overlapped when working the dubbed tying thread along the shank.

To attach the fur to the thread, hold the thread out from the hook. Take a small pinch of fur between the forefinger and thumb of the other hand. Slip the tying thread between this forefinger and thumb. Then slide these two fingers over each other thus spinning the fur onto the thread. Always slide the forefinger and thumb in the same direction. Reversing the slide only untwists the fur (Figure 9.8).

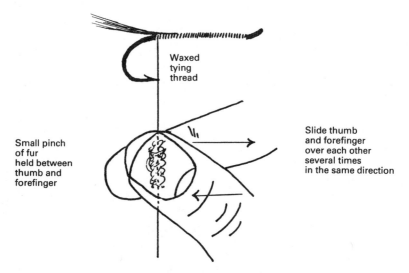

Waxed
tying
thread

Small pinch
of fur
held between
thumb and
forefinger

Slide thumb
and forefinger
over each other
several times
in the same direction

Figure 9.8. Dubbing fur bodies.

Natural fur is often a subtle blend of several shades. Dyed fur tends to be uniform in shade. When the latter is used, especially in bold colours, the finished body can look a little harsh and unnatural. This is simply a matter of taste but I prefer to mix furs of different shades and from different animals, just enough to mellow the colour a little.

A slightly more time consuming method of dubbing which can be applied to hackle fibres, marabou and hair as well as fur is as follows. Rub some extra wax onto the tying thread as it hangs from the hook. Make a loop of tying thread around your forefinger and secure this to the hook with several turns of thread. Place a wire hook onto this 'dubbing loop' and hold the loop open with your forefinger. Slide some dubbing material into the loop and gently remove your finger. The hook is pulled to tighten the waxed thread onto the dubbing. The hook is then spun between forefinger and thumb. This twists the thread, spinning the dubbing material and gripping it. It is then wound around the hook to make a body or hackle which is translucent, mobile and very attractive. When made with hare, rabbit or even teddy bear fur this is a good alternative to the soft game hackle on my SBs.

In my box of seal's fur and synthetic dubbing I keep several packets of mixing fur: guard hairs from hare and rabbit and grey under fur from hare, rabbit and mole. Each of these fur types can be blended with any colour of dubbing fur to achieve a more mellow lifelike effect. The mole is perhaps a little more difficult to mix than the others because of its fine texture but is still useful. Only a very little of a mixing is required.

There are two ways of mixing fur dubbing — mechanical and manual. We must also consider the types of fur to be mixed. Where possible choose furs of similar texture so that an even mix is easier to achieve. The procedure for blending mole fur with coarser fibres is to lay out the seal on a white piece of paper and sprinkle tiny pieces of mole over it as evenly as possible. Then fold all the fur into a bunch. Pull this bunch apart, place the two halves together and repeat it several times making sure that as pieces of fur fall they are picked up and replaced in the bunch.

This method is more successful when mixing the guard hairs of rabbit or hare to seal as their texture is more alike. A coffee grinder will mix fur very well but is, in my opinion, most unnecessary as the manual method is quite adequate.

The aforementioned furs are the most commonly used, but do not be restricted. There are plenty more easily available to the flytier, not only those bought in tackle shops. Experiment is invaluable and has lead to several famous patterns. It is said that the original Tups Indispensable mixture contained dog hair and several more unsavoury items. The possibilities are endless.

Raffia

Many fly dressers suggest wetting certain materials in order to obtain the correct set or appearance on the fly. Raffia is one of the few materials which needs to be wet during tying. I have found wetting other materials of very little value. If a part of the fly requires saliva to hold it in place it shows one of two things: poor choice of material or poor workmanship. In any event the set is not likely to last. Raffia is the exception which proves the rule, it must always be wet when tied in. When wet raffia is pulled tight all creases are removed and the result is a silky smooth body.

Natural raffia is most common on traditional Mayfly and Daddy Long Legs patterns. Both often have tapered bodies, thickset near the head. It is wrong to achieve this with several layers of overlapping raffia. After successive use and drying out it is too easy for the layers to slip over each other. A tapered underbody of straw or yellow-coloured floss silk is better, with a single raffia layer over the top.

Some form of rib is useful for durability but varnish below will only discolour the finished body.

Raffiene is a synthetic and more reflective material but in all other aspects it is treated exactly as raffia. Both are tied in just the same way as were the previous materials. Raffiene is more frequently used for backs of flies, for example, Polystickles.

The main drawback of raffia and raffiene, as far as I am concerned, is that both materials tend to soften when wet which often leads to durability problems.

Deer hair

Deer hair is a relatively modern material in flytying terms. Flotation is the prime reason for its use for bodies. There are two methods of applying it for different uses.

It can be spun onto the hook in one or several bunches and trimmed to produce two totally different flies: G & H Sedge and heads of Muddler Minnows, both formed in the same way. In the first example it is not really a body material at all. It is spun onto the hook along the length of the shank and trimmed to give both flotation and profile of the sedge wing. The body is composed of seal's fur dubbed onto a separate length of thread and stretched below the hook (Figure 9.7).

The G & H sedge is included here because it is applied in exactly the same method as the Muddler Minnow head. Cut a small bunch of deer hair from the skin. Hold the fibres by the tips and, using your fingers, flick the cut ends several times to remove the fine fluff nearest the deer's skin. Place this bunch on top of the hook preferably over a bare hook or as little previous dressing as possible. With the deer hair held all round the hook, make two or three loose turns of a preferably strong — Naples silk or monocord — thread around the deer hair and hook. Slowly pull the thread tight and at the same time gradually remove the fingers which are gripping the hair. The deer hair should spin around the hook as the thread tightens and splay out in all directions. It may be necessary to make another turn or two as you tighten. It will immediately become clear why the bunch of hair must be small. Too big a bunch will simply not work. Note that when the deer hair is secure the thread is brought through it towards the eye of the hook to tie off or continue the dressing. A small drop of varnish or superglue can be used to prevent further slipping. A small drop is allowed to run along from the eye down to the base of the fibres. Very little must be used to avoid the whole hair being soaked. The hair is then trimmed to the desired shape and size. Deer hair is also used to make some caterpillar bodies and the head of Collyer's hatching midge pupae. It is a slightly tricky process to perform at first, but the most difficult part is not so much the tying but the trimming. Usually a great deal of deer hair must be removed (Figure 9.9).

Small bunch
of deer hair
all around hook.
Several loose
turns of thread.
Hold deer hair
lightly and
pull thread downwards

The deer hair
fans out in
all directions.
The thread is
wound to the
eye. Then whip
finish

The deer hair is
trimmed with
razor blade or
scissors. Then a small
drop of varnish
secures the dressing

Figure 9.9. Spinning deer hair for bodies and heads.

There is a simpler method of making a deer hair body appropriate to some sedges, and pupae. A small bunch of hair is tied on top of the hook near the eye. This spreads out to give the impression of emerging wings (Plates 2 and 8). When this is repeated all around the shank it is a useful technique for making Muddler-style heads especially around bead chain eyes. Deer hair may also be laid along the shank and tied in at the bend and the eye. To do this place the bunch around the hook and tie it in at the tail. Then pull the fibres back over the bend and bring the thread to the eye and bind in the fibres to the hook again. A rib of tinsel or thread may be used to add strength to this type of body. It is not always necessary to trim off all the ends; leaving some of the fibres at either end may add an impression of life, especially with hatching insects.

Paint

Silver paint was the original dressing Hugh Falkus used for the body of the Medicine fly. I frequently use this fly but I have never found any success with the paint in terms of durability so I never use it now. My preference is for flat mylar tinsel over a fine strong monocord and ribbed with fine wire, with the possible addition of superglue. This makes the dressing slim enough, shinier and more durable than paint.

Luminous paint is sometimes suggested as a useful body material for sea trout flies. I doubt that it has any beneficial effect over tinsel and I strongly suspect it might have distinct fish repellant qualities. Decide for yourself. The important thing for luminous body materials, especially paint, is to have an underbody. It must be white. White tying thread will do but it is not ideal. A better finish is gained by winding a strip of white plastic (from a supermarket carrier bag) over the thread, then applying paint on top.

Luminous tape is available but as it also requires a white underbody, the result is a significantly fatter body. It is much less messy though and the fly is finished at one sitting. By partly overlapping the turns of tape a ridged effect is obtained.

Silver hook

Undressed, silver hook makes the above Medicine-style fly very much easier though I still lean towards the ordinary hook and tinsel. The reason being that the bend point and barb are just as bright as the body. I believe, without any good evidence to back it up, that if the fly dressing appears to be separate from the hook and the bend, etc. the fly will have less chance of being ignored by the fish.

Balsa or cork

Small pieces of balsa or cork impaled and glued to wire or nylon line, sanded to the correct shape and painted can successfully reproduce the profile of some terrestrial flies. Such material also has the advantage of being able to float. Beetles, grasshoppers, ants, American-style crickets and so on can all be made in this way. Even floating freshwater snails can be shaped from balsa or cork, if you are not satisifed with the Black and Peacock spider (Plate 4). There are enormous possibilities, but the terrestrial flies made in this way are of only limited importance in the United Kingdom.

Cork really comes into its own when used for a sea trout surface lure. Using a hot needle, simply burn a hole through a small cork (or a trimmed down wine cork). Twist elasticum trace wire onto a swivel through the cork and add a few small beads to keep the hook a little behind the cork. Attach a treble hook to the wire, bind it down tight with thread and soak the binding in superglue. Paint the cork silver or black to taste (Figure 9.13).

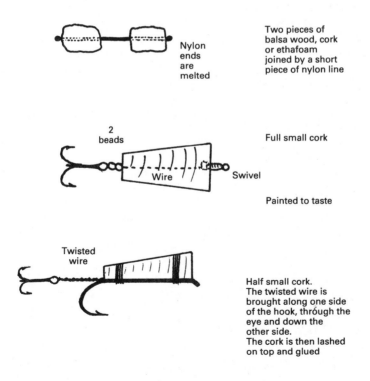

Figure 9.13. Balsa or cork bodies.

Quill

Some of the original surface lures created by Hugh Falkus were made using the ends of quills sealed up with cork or balsa, with pieces of feather lashed to each side as stabilizers. The whole assembly was then bound to an appropriate mount.

It is also possible to create a passable representation of a caterpillar from a smaller section of finer quill. The fibres on each side of the tip of a goose wing, quill or similar feather, are snipped roughly and dyed to brown or green. The resulting lifeless looking stick is tied and glued to a long shank hook. It is maybe a little stiff looking but the profile can be excellent.

Sand and Gravel

It sounds most unlikely but if carefully applied these materials can make a remarkable caddis larva lookalike. Take a long shank hook and wrap an underbody of copper wire roughly around the shank. This is certainly an example of when it pays to be untidy. The turns — overlapping and very uneven — should be anything but neat. The reason is that a rough underbody adds grip to the sand or gravel which is glued on top. To do this cover the whole assembly in superglue. When this is dry, coat the hook with rubber glue, dip it in sand and when dry give it a top coat of superglue. Even with this, little bits will drop off in use but its application will help to extend the life of the body (Figure 9.14).

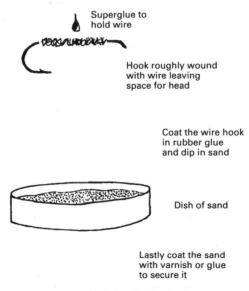

Figure 9.14. Sand/gravel body.

If gravel is used you must try to avoid blocking too much of the hook's gape or its hooking qualities will be reduced. The material used will depend on the type of sedge fly found in a particular water. Even pieces of dried grass and twig can be used but the lifespan of these is even shorter.

Tube flies and Waddington shanks are usually dressed with bodies exactly the same as the standard salmon fly body. But tube flies can be even easier than that. Simply tie on a hair wing all round the tube and omit the body dressing altogether. Many leading names in the sport do this and they stick with the method because it works. It should be noted that to secure the hair properly a very short bed of waxed thread is still as important as with any other fly, to stop the dressing from slipping.

It really does not seem of any importance to many experienced salmon anglers whether their hair-winged flies have bodies at all. Tubes of brass, copper, aluminium, plastic and even ordinary black hook, undressed except for a hair wing seem to be perfectly acceptable to the fish (Plate 14).

Detached bodies

A realistic body effect for dry flies is obtained by tying a bunch of deer hair together away from the hook, on a needle, which is removed after tying. Use thread of an appropriate colour, normally brown. Bind the fibres together at one end, use the same thread to rib the body and bind the other end tightly to the hook (Figure 9.10). Then varnish the body lightly. As a detached body it is useful for Mayflies or Daddy Long Legs. For the Mayfly it is a good idea to leave several long fibres as a tail or have the tail material (such as cock pheasant centre tail fibres) embedded within the body. It is an interesting technique but seldom used.

An easier detached body is the readymade 'Poly Body'. This is a plastic tube which is already moulded to shape. It is easy and effective, but always remember when a hole is punched in it for the tail fibres, a small drop of varnish is required to seal the end so that the body retains its ability to float. One problem with this type of body is the bulkiness of the tie-in point of the hook. This may have to be hidden.

A very interesting method of making a detached body, which has the added advantage of being virtually unsinkable, is that which uses a rubber-based glue. It is perhaps most appropriate for Daddy Long Legs (Plate 10) or Mayflies but could also be employed on other flies which must be fished on the surface. Simply smear a thin film of rubber-based glue on any flat surface, wait until it is dry then push the edge with a finger to roll up the glue. The amount rolled naturally determines its thickness. Colour can be added by waterproof felt-tip pens before rolling. Tails may be added while the glue film is rolled. Very simple and tremendously lifelike and effective (Figure 9.11).

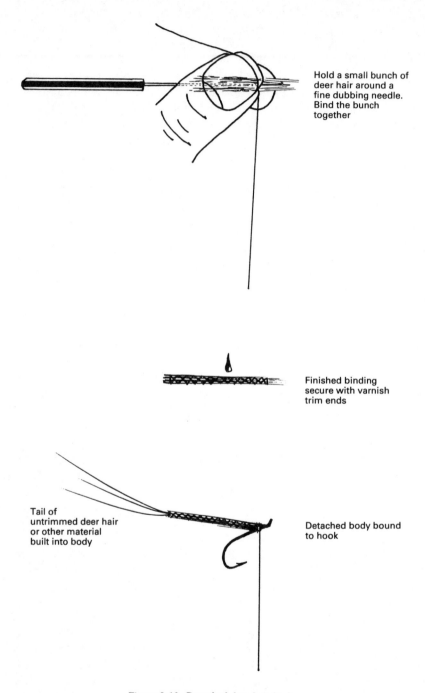

Hold a small bunch of
deer hair around a
fine dubbing needle.
Bind the bunch
together

Finished binding
secure with varnish
trim ends

Tail of
untrimmed deer hair
or other material
built into body

Detached body bound
to hook

Figure 9.10. Detached deer hair body.

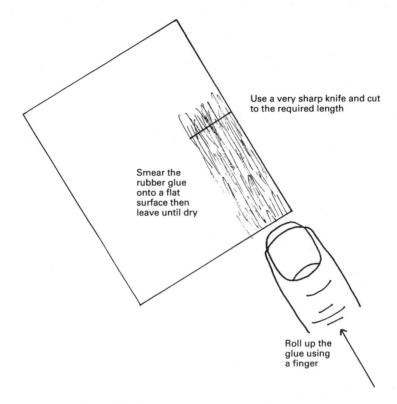

Use a very sharp knife and cut
to the required length

Smear the
rubber glue
onto a flat
surface then
leave until dry

Roll up the
glue using
a finger

Figure 9.11. Using a rubber based glue to form a body.

A variation on the idea of detached bodies, but this time used for wet
flies, is the Wiggle Nymph. This is mainly used for large nymphs, for
example the Damsel fly.

I prefer to use a straight-eyed hook for the rear part of the body. The
bend of the hook is nipped off with pliers and the hook held in the vice by
the eye; the tail, body and ribbing are then tied on. The main problem here
is to get used to the fact that, for right-handed ties, the tail is tied at the end
of the hook which is at the right-hand side instead of at the left as normal.
When the rear section is finished a piece of wire or nylon is threaded
through the eye and fixed to the front hook in the same way as the
construction of a tandem mount (Figure 21.1). The mount should therefore
be articulated in the middle, the rest of the fly being tied on to the front
hook.

An alternative method is to tie the dressing on to the rear hook before
the bend is nipped off. Both methods work perfectly well — the former is
neater whereas the latter is quicker (Fig 9.12).

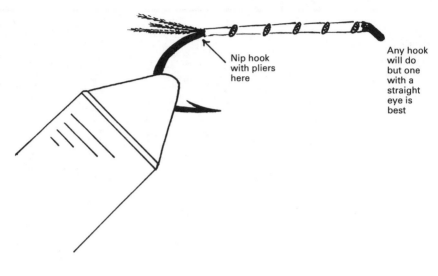

Body tied in usual way

Nip hook
with pliers
here

Any hook
will do
but one
with a
straight
eye is
best

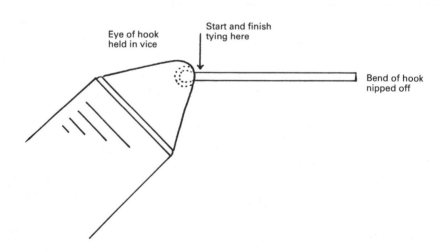

Eye of hook
held in vice

Start and finish
tying here

Bend of hook
nipped off

Figure 9.12. Rear part of articulated body.

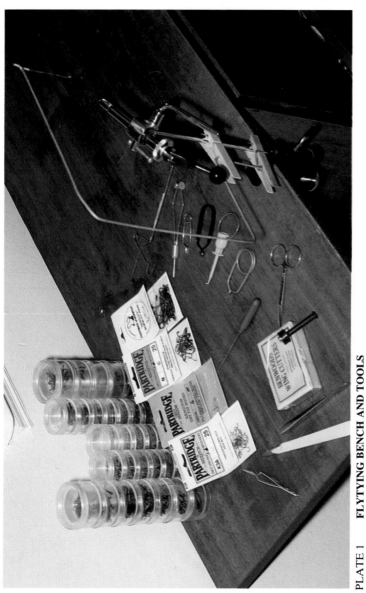

PLATE 1 **FLYTYING BENCH AND TOOLS**
Vice
Homemade gallows
Scissors
Dubbing needle
Selection of hackle pliers

Whip finish tool
Bobbin holder
Scalpel
Wing pliers
Wing cutters

Tweezers
Hooks in regular use in stack-packs
Specialised hooks in packets

PLATE 2 *(see page 148)*

SBs FOR LOCH TROUT
Four representatives of the SB style of trout fly. Almost any standard wet or dry fly pattern may be reformed in this style and in doing so you will almost certainly improve its fishing qualities.

The table of patterns offers a few suggestions on which to base experiments.

PLATE 3 *(see page 148)*

SBs FOR SEA TROUT AND SALMON
Examples of the SB idea designed to be fished on an even keel. I prefer bronze mallard because it is about as close as a feather can come to a hair wing, but teal and similar feathers are also useful.

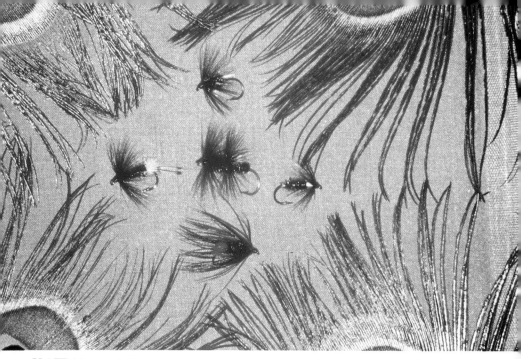

PLATE 4 *(see page 148)*

PEACOCK FLIES

Never go fishing for trout without at least one peacock fly in your box. Peacock herl has always been one of the most versatile and attractive materials available to the flytier. These are my favourites but there are hundreds to choose from.

PLATE 5 *(see page 149)*

LIFELESS FLIES

There is no doubt that these patterns are highly successful for many anglers, but they have little in-built translucency or mobility. I often hold a few such patterns in reserve but for my fishing they are rarely used.

REPRESENTATIVE FLIES

Each pattern in this series of plates is an attempt to represent one of the major items on the trout's menu. Each type occurs in a variety of colours depending on the time of year, area of the country and type of water. There are tables of insects, their seasons and colours but I have never found these to be very accurate. It is for the angler to learn by experience or advice which is best in his area during the season.

No such pattern can ever be an exact copy of a natural insect. The flies on these plates demonstrate varying degrees of realism and caricature. During a hatch I generally look for a pattern which is similar to the natural but with some feature which is intended to make the artificial stand out from the crowd. No matter how lifelike an artificial might be there is no guarantee that the fish take it for the 'right' reason.

PLATE 7 *(see page 149)*   PLATE 8 *(see page 149)*

Top — PLATE 9 *(see page 149)*   Below — PLATE 10 *(see page 150)*

PLATE 11 *(see page 150)*

GENERAL WET FLIES

Although the backbone of my trout and sea trout armoury consists of various forms of SB no single style of fly can cover all situations. These are a few extras which I have found useful for loch trout, sea trout and as droppers for salmon. The 'flying' single hook on the Trident is cheaper, often stronger and just as effective as a treble.

PLATE 12 *(see page 150)*

LURES

All flies are lures but this word is usually associated with large gaudy rainbow trout flies. I have included these patterns because they are quick and simple to tie and they have also caught brown or sea trout for me when used in appropriate sizes.

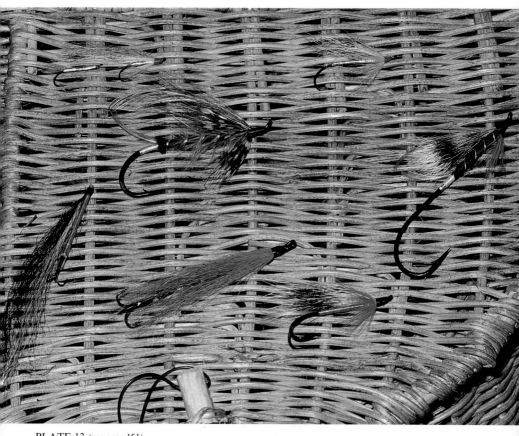

PLATE 13 *(see page 151)*

LARGE SALMON AND SEA TROUT FLIES
These patterns are popular, successful and illustrate varying degrees of simplicity in the tying.
What is wrong with some of these is the mounts on which they are tied. Waddingtons and
tubes have taken over from the massive Thunder and Lightning meat hook because of their
better hooking qualities. The Collie Dog achieves length and weight but keeps the hook well
away from the tail for fish taking the lure by the head. Few low-water patterns were ever used
this big but this style of fly is generally being replaced by small double and treble hooked flies.
I use doubles for most of my salmon flies but this hook is too big — leverage on either side of
this hook could seriously weaken its grip. Sea trout flies like the Medicine should often be
large but it is usually better to use some form of tandem mount rather than the single.

PLATE 14 *(see page 151)*

SMALL SALMON AND SEA TROUT FLIES
Modern summer salmon flies are simple with small hooks, usually doubles and trebles. The double hooks ensure that the fly keeps on an even keel but with the trebles this does not matter. Slimness is an important quality of most salmon flies but in very slack water I prefer short bushy flies like the treble. In this situation larger slim flies need to be retrieved to keep them level in the water. The wee double has largely taken over from the low-water style. The long-shank treble and the tubes show variations in slimness, weight and quantity of dressing.

PLATE 15 *(see page 151)*

SALMON SHRIMPS/PRAWNS
All these patterns, in some way, are intended to be suggestive of shrimps and prawns. The
more traditional forms in terms of movement with modern versions which look more realistic.
Again double hooks are preferred both for fishing qualities and ease of tying. The hackle on
the realistic pattern tends to act like a parachute making the fly 'swim' upside-down even
when the hook is weighted, but it is still a deadly fly in some areas. The Waddington was an
attempt to ensure that none of the dressing hung behind the hook. This pattern landed my
only salmon to date in pitch darkness.

PLATE 16

VARIATIONS ON A SALMON SHRIMP

Angling books and magazines are full of 'new' flies with new names which are merely variations on existing patterns. This plate shows a few ways in which a single pattern can be modified.

Either the material is identical to the original (top) and the tying method is slightly altered, or substitute materials such as marabou and squirrel tail are used. The possibilities are almost limitless.

Incidentally, traditional salmon shrimps tied on trout hooks are excellent rainbow trout lures.

These brown trout were caught in West Highland hill lochs. The top one with an SB *(see plate 2)* and the bottom one with a duck fly *(see plate 6)*. *(Photographs by Mike Shanks)*

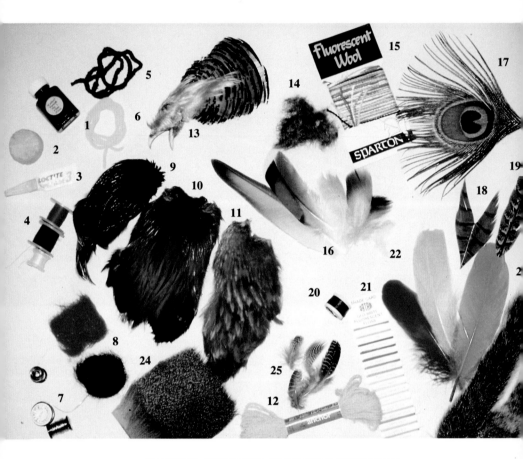

PLATE 17 ESSENTIAL AND USEFUL MATERIALS

(a) ESSENTIAL MATERIALS

1. Clear Varnish
2. Solid wax
3. Superglue
4. Red, black and yellow tying thread
5. Chenille
6. Fluorescent chenille
7. Selection of wires, tinsels, ovals
8. Seal's fur sub
9. Dyed cock capes
10. Natural cock capes
11. Natural hen capes
12. Embroidery wool
13. Golden pheasant crest and tippet
14. Hare fur
15. Fluorescent wool

16. Male mallard feathers – wing breast flank tail
17. Peacock tail feather
18. Cock pheasant tail
19. Hen pheasant tail
20. Marabou floss silk
21. Fluorescent floss
22. Goose shoulder feathers – various colours
23. Squirrel tail natural and dyed
24. Deer hair
25. Selection of soft hackles from – Partridge Grouse Teal Waterhen

(b) USEFUL MATERIALS

1. Bucktail dyed in a range of colours	12. Mole fur
2. Calf tail dyed in a range of colours	13. Marabou plumes
3. Synthetic dubbing	14. Raffiene
4. Flexibody	15. Turkey tail
5. Lureflash Mobile	16. Peacock sword
6. Lureflash Crystal hair	17. Peacock blue neck
7. Lureflash Twinkle	18. Antron yarn standard and fluorescent
8. Dyed deer hair	19. Starling full skin
9. Rabbit fur	20. Guinea fowl dyed blue
10. Black ostrich herl	21. Blue jay
11. Golden pheasant body	

PLATE 18   UNNECESSARY AND UNORTHODOX MATERIALS

I have included this 'unnecessary' list because all such materials are available and regularly described in other books as either essential or useful. They are neither, in practical fish-catching terms, because there are cheaper and more easily obtainable substitutes and alternatives which are in some cases more 'environmentally friendly'.

(a)   UNNECESSARY MATERIALS

1. Badger hair
2. Goat hair
3. Stoat's tail
4. Mylar piping
5. Natural seal's fur
6. Toucan sub
7. Indian crow sub
8. Kingfisher
9. 'Highest-quality' cock capes
10. Amherst pheasant tippet and crest
11. Jungle cock
12. Barred wood duck
13. French partridge hackle
14. Heron wing quill
15. Swan
16. Macaw
17. Florican bustard

(b) UNORTHODOX MATERIALS

1. Pullover for dubbing
2. Plastic folder
3. Budgie feather
4. Canary feather
5. Lead foil from wine bottle
6. Copper electrical wire
7. Paint brush
8. 'Hair' and dubbing from a variety of dolls
9. Human hair
10. Rubber glue
11. Surgical glove
12. Foil crisp packet
13. Audio tape
14. Foam packing material
15. Christmas tinsel
16. Stocking material
17. Lurex on spindle from craft shop

Rainbow trout from a 'put and take fishery' caught on a cat's whisker *(see plate 12)*.
(Photograph by Mike Shanks)

This salmon was taken from a West Highland spate river on a Shanks' purple shrimp *(see plate 15)*.
(Photograph by Mike Shanks)

10 Hackles

There is a great variety of feathers and furs suitable for use as hackles, and many ways of tying them. Most common are cock and hen hackles tied as a collar around the hook close to the eye. It is important, as with all aspects of construction, to choose materials with regard to the effect required. Much has been written on the subject of hackle quality, particularly cock hackles for dry flies. The result has been the introduction of cock capes with perfect feathers costing ten times that of the standard cape. I have used these and they are excellent, but it hardly seems worth the expense to me (Plate 18). Over a number of years I have done well in competitions for all types of fly, including dry fly, using moderately-priced capes.

No matter which type of hackle is used the first step is to pick one with the correct length of fibre or flue. In this way a hackle is chosen for either functional or aesthetic reasons. In representations of a natural insect, the former is paramount but on traditional wet flies, salmon flies and the like, the latter is more important.

Size, set or angle of fibres to the body, and degree of movement are the considerations for a natural if a realistic enough caricature is to be made. An ephemeroptera nymph may have a very short hackle of hen. Sometimes it may only have the thorax fur picked out as with some tyings of the Gold-Ribbed Hare's Ear. A spider pattern with a very soft hackle of partridge can be suggestive of ephemeroptera nymphs, provided that it has a very much longer hackle which represents body profile and tail when wet and pulled through the water.

Strip away the down or 'fluff' and a few of the base fibres from the hackle. Leave only the best quality fibres; this may mean removing more fibres than you expect but it is not wasteful if the finished fly has the desired qualities.

The hackle must then be tied in with as few turns of thread as possible, perhaps even using the method described earlier (see Figure 4.1).

A hackle may be tied in one of two ways: by the tip, or by the stalk end of the feather (Figure 10.1). For cock and hen hackles there may be little to choose between tip or stalk but for soft hackles such as partridge, grouse and golden pheasant breast the feather should always be tied in by the tip. Even for cock and hen hackles the following points should be considered.

The tip end is the one most likely to break. So, if the stalk end is tied in first and the tip does break merely grip the hackle with the hackle pliers a little further down the stalk.

The length of the hackle fibres usually increases towards the base end of the stalk. This is true of most hackles but not all. Hen hackles are one of the main exceptions. When a cock hackle is being wound at the shoulder it

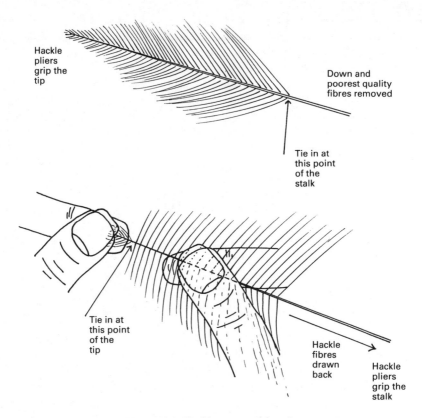

Hackle
pliers
grip the
tip

Down and
poorest quality
fibres removed

Tie in at
this point
of the
stalk

Tie in at
this point
of the
tip

Hackle
fibres
drawn
back

Hackle
pliers
grip the
stalk

Figure 10.1. Hackles prepared for tying.

might be thought useful to tie it in by the tip. Then, as the hackle is wound
for several turns towards the eye, the longer fibres will lie over the shorter
ones. This may enhance the appearance of the fly but nothing else.

If durability is considered important for a bushy fly an addition can be
made to the above. By the time the first few turns are made towards the
eye not only should the fibres be a little longer, but also the hackle stalk
will be thicker and stronger. Make a turn or two back through the hackle
turns already made; work towards the tail and back again to the eye where
it is tied off (Figure 10.2).

Some flytiers wind the hackle in front of the hanging thread and others
wind the thread through the hackle — take your pick. I find the first
method ideal for me and it can be strengthened by a tiny drop of varnish at
the base of the fibres. For wet flies the root of the hackle is also made more
secure when giving it the required set (i.e. the hackle points pointing back
a little towards the tail). This, rather than having a sweep's brush

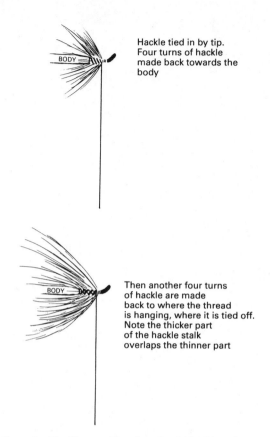

Hackle tied in by tip.
Four turns of hackle
made back towards the
body

Then another four turns
of hackle are made
back to where the thread
is hanging, where it is tied off.
Note the thicker part
of the hackle stalk
overlaps the thinner part

Figure 10.2. Winding a hackle. Note position for tying in hackle a few turns in front of the finished body.

appearance required for many dry flies. The turn or two of thread which secures this may overlap the base of the fibres, which ensures a stronger construction.

Some hackles are naturally more difficult to use than others. The soft hackle of grouse and partridge (mostly the latter) are so fine that extreme delicacy is required if the feather is not to be broken. There are even softer hackles — I have used back feathers from a blackbird in a successful version of the Black and Peacock spider. All such hackles are tied in by the tip.

No matter which soft hackle is used the operation is always the same. Hold the tip fibres firmly and draw the rest very gently backwards towards the stalk end. The tip is then tied in and the hackle wound (Figure 10.3). Hackle fibres can be 'doubled' before tying, but I have found this to be both time consuming and unnecessary (Figure 10.3).

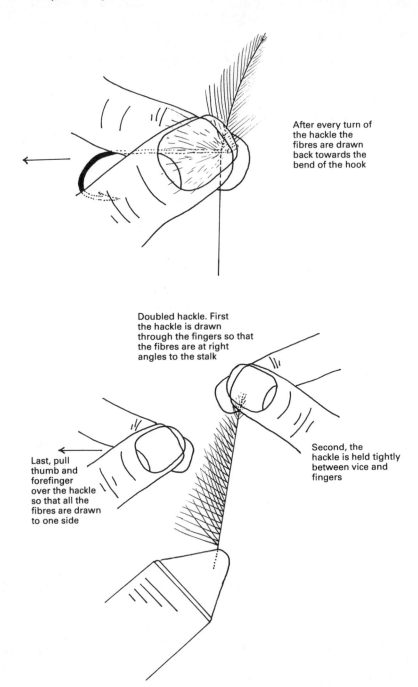

After every turn of
the hackle the
fibres are drawn
back towards the
bend of the hook

Doubled hackle. First
the hackle is drawn
through the fingers so that
the fibres are at right
angles to the stalk

Last, pull
thumb and
forefinger
over the hackle
so that all the
fibres are drawn
to one side

Second, the
hackle is held tightly
between vice and
fingers

Figure 10.3. Drawing back hackle fibres and doubling hackle.

Some hackles have the opposite problem — being too strong. For example, a blue jay wing feather which has been substituted by blue-dyed guinea fowl, doubtless because of tying difficulties, which is a pity. To tie a wound jay hackle is not easy and takes a lot of time. First, the stalk of the feather must be greatly reduced in bulk, having come from the wing of the bird rather than the neck. A very sharp knife is required to split the stalk. As much of the stalk as possible must be removed and the spongy core must be scraped away with the point of the knife. Even when this is done the stalk will take up a lot of room between the body and the eye when winding. It is quite possible that several feathers will be wasted before this operation can be done adequately. It is therefore not surprising that the very much easier guinea fowl has taken the place of the blue jay.

However, there is a very simple solution which can also be employed for partridge and grouse hackles, etc. especially useful when a short-fibred hackle is required. Simply tear off a bunch of fibres from a suitable feather. Make sure that the tips of the fibres are arranged so that they are of equal length. As soon as the thread is wound onto the hook at the beginning of tying, tie in the bunch of fibres so that they are evenly distributed around the shank and the points of the fibres reach over the eye of the hook. It is very easy to ensure that the correct hackle length is achieved. Tie the blunt ends of the fibres along the shank as the thread is wound down to the tail. These ends can be trimmed at an angle to help produce a tapered body. When the body is finished, draw the hackle fibres back towards the tail and bring the thread through them. With a turn or two the correct set of the fibres can be ensured (Figure 10.4).

Bunch of hackle fibres tied in at the beginning

When the rest of the fly is tied the hackle fibres are pulled back and the head is made

Figure 10.4. 'Bunch of fibres' hackle.

This method also helps to make a small neat head which is very difficult for a wound jay hackle. This is a method which I have used to good effect on my own pattern, the Trident (Plate 11).

Dry fly hackles require reasonably good quality feathers but, as already stated, it is unnecessary to pay a fortune for them. However, with lower quality feathers I have found it useful to use two hackles instead of one. This can have several effects one of which is that with three or four turns of each of the hackles a very buoyant fly is produced; or, if you do not have the required shade of hackle, two hackles of complementary colour can give the same effect, for example, black and cream hackles together are a substitute for badger hackles. If the two hackle feathers have very different lengths of fibre one could be tied in by the tip, the other by the end of the stalk. These are wound one through the other. The lengths of the fibres of each feather are thus mixed and the poor quality is hidden.

Two hackles together can also be used in wet flies with good results. If a very soft hackle (like blackbird body feather) is used in some situations it may lie so close to the body, especially in fast water, that its movement is lost and so is the impression of life. It may help to add a turn or two of a suitably coloured cock hackle before the soft hackle is wound on. I have conducted a few such experiments with interesting but inconclusive results. I merely suggest it may be worth a try. When the cock hackle is fixed, wind it so that the hackle points are directed over the eye and not, as is normal, leaning towards the tail. When the softer hackle is added and set pointing tailwards the fibres interlock producing an attractive impression in the water (Figure 10.5).

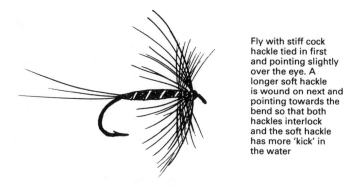

Fly with stiff cock hackle tied in first and pointing slightly over the eye. A longer soft hackle is wound on next and pointing towards the bend so that both hackles interlock and the soft hackle has more 'kick' in the water

Figure 10.5. Two hackles together.

A similar idea came from the observation, which surely we have all made, that feather wings, particularly on the standard wet fly seldom last intact for long. No matter how well tied or carefully handled, it is all too common for the fibres of the wing to split. The fish's view of such a fly is certainly not going to be what we see as the fly sits finished in the vice. Why not tie a fly with this very common tattiness built in?

Take a Blae and Black as an example. This is so often used and so often attacked by trout that although the feathers remain secure, the fly loses its original profile. Often just such a fly is more successful than a fresh one. Why then do we not use the wing material as a hackle in the same fashion as jay is used for the Trident? (Plate 11).

An Invicta (Plate 11) is another good example. It also is regularly used, but also may represent a hatching sedge where as much movement as possible should be an advantage and the winging material, hen pheasant tail, is very prone to splitting. Changing the wing to a hackle is not appropriate for all flies, only on those where a standard wing profile is not essential should it be tried (See Part 2 and Plate 2).

Throat, Beard or False Hackle — whatever you call it the result is much the same. These hackles, in my opinion, should only be used when slimness is of paramount importance and mobility less so. I try to avoid them where possible because although they are simple to tie they are lifeless compared to a sparsely-dressed collar hackle and have a much more stark appearance. One situation where they are ideal is with low-water salmon flies where slimness and lack of dressing produce a very attractive effect.

First, pick the appropriate feather which should have fibres of equal length on each side of the stalk. Cut through the stalk at close intervals so that you have three or four pieces of stalk with the fibres attached. Place these one on top of each other so that the fibre tips are even. The number of pieces depends on the requirements of the fly construction and your own personal preference (Figure 10.6).

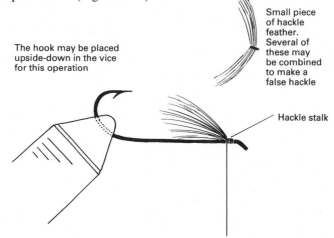

The hook may be placed upside-down in the vice for this operation

Small piece of hackle feather. Several of these may be combined to make a false hackle

Hackle stalk

Figure 10.6. False or Beard hackle during construction.

You can if you wish turn the hook upside-down in the vice for this. I rarely bother. Turning the hook upside-down has the advantage of making it easier to ensure that the fibres do not lean to one side. This is important, not just for appearance but to keep the hook in the right position in the water. So, whatever method you use, check it before tying any further. It certainly helps if your vice will allow the fly to be turned upside-down without releasing the hook. One way to get over the problem of over-sparseness (if a fly can suffer from such a thing), is to ensure that, at the point of tying in, the fibres are not cramped on one point of the bottom of the hook shank but arranged to spread out around the bottom half of the hook shank (Figure 10.7).

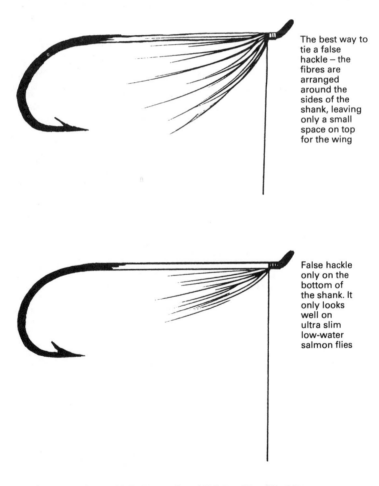

The best way to tie a false hackle – the fibres are arranged around the sides of the shank, leaving only a small space on top for the wing

False hackle only on the bottom of the shank. It only looks well on ultra slim low-water salmon flies

Figure 10.7. Two styles of False or Beard hackle.

Like everything else there is no right or wrong way to tie a Palmer hackle over the body of a fly. But different methods may be easier or more secure or more appropriate to the required effect. As ever, experiment is useful.

Method 1

Old Palmer method — when the body of the fly is complete and the thread hangs vertically down from the hook tie in the hackle by the stalk. Wind it evenly down the body and back again through the hackle already wound on (about four turns in each direction should do). The ribbing material, if any, is then wound evenly along the body and through the hackle fibres and fixed at the same position as the hackle. This produces a very bushy body hackle with the body partly obscured. It can be a little untidy because when winding rib and hackle through the fibres it is too easy to trap the hackle fibres against the body. But the result is a very durable construction (see Figure 7.1b).

Method 2

I do not like this method much because I have found it to have some durability problems (see Figure 7.1a). However, it is similar to the old Palmer method, but less bushy, in that it uses only four to five turns of hackle — this is an advantage because few hackles (unless one is paying a fortune) have eight turns of good fibre on them.

Do exactly as with the old Palmer method but stop when four to five turns have been made. Let the hackle pliers hold the hackle by their weight at the tail. As the hackle hangs, wind the rib through it for about the same number of turns to the head and finish in the usual way. Trim off the hackle, flush to the body of the fly.

Method 3

This is another method of tying a body hackle using about the same amount of feather as already described in Method 2 above. Done correctly, it should be much neater than either of the two previous methods. It is the method I use most, but you must decide where neatness comes in your list of priorities and pick your method accordingly.

After the tail or butt (if any) has been tied in, secure a hackle by the tip. To do this, hold the hackle in the hackle pliers by the tip and gently draw the fibres back towards the root of the stalk. One turn should be enough to hold the hackle because body or ribbing material may also be tied at the same point. The hackle tip should not be trimmed but left under the body. The body and ribbing are wound on. Then the hackle is wound along the body tight in to the ribbing and just to the tail side of it. If the ribbing is of oval it should give sufficient protection to the hackle stalk. Many books on flytying suggest that hackles tied in this way should be doubled before tying in the hackle point. The idea is that the fibres should be wetted and folded, using the fingers, so as to be on one side of the stalk (Figure 10.3). As already stated, I find no advantage in this process. When the hackle is wound close enough to the ribbing the result is just that which is required.

If you prefer Method 3 as I do but need a bushier fly like a bumble, simply tie in two hackles by the tips and wind them both together as before. To do this hackle pliers should not be used; winding with the finger tips will help to keep both hackles evenly tight. This way there will be no problem of hackle fibres being crushed onto the body by the ribbing. Depending on the degree of bushiness required, any of these three methods may be used. But if even the third method is too bushy, simply remove the fibres from one side of the hackle before tying in. The result is a very sparse hackle. This is a technique which is also used to good effect with soft hackles of teal or mallard breast when wound as a collar. This does not only give a sparse dressing but also a much neater one with all the fibres pointing towards the tail (see Figure 7.1d).

Method 4

A half-bodied hackle is also a useful way to suggest a hatching dun. The process is the same as for the old Palmer method, except that only about two turns need be wound down the body and back again.

Alternatively, tie in the hackle by the point half-way up the shank as the thread is wound back towards the eye. Wind the body material and ribbing, if any, around the hackle. When the body is complete a couple of turns of hackle should bring it to the head. This method is also used on some salmon flies: here it is important that the ribbing, on its second or third turn, should meet the hackle tie-in point under the shank.

Parachute hackles have come into vogue again in recent years. This is largely as a result of the publication of the excellent book *The Trout and the Fly* (1980) by Brian Clarke and John Goddard. The parachute hackle style has the reputation of being difficult — I don't know why. It often requires an extra gadget, a Gallows and it does take longer than the usual method but is not too difficult.

The idea behind a parachute hackle is that the hackle of a dry fly should not penetrate the water but rest on the surface to give a much more realistic impression of an insect's legs in the surface film. Also, the hook may not penetrate the surface — particularly when the fly is tied upside-down.

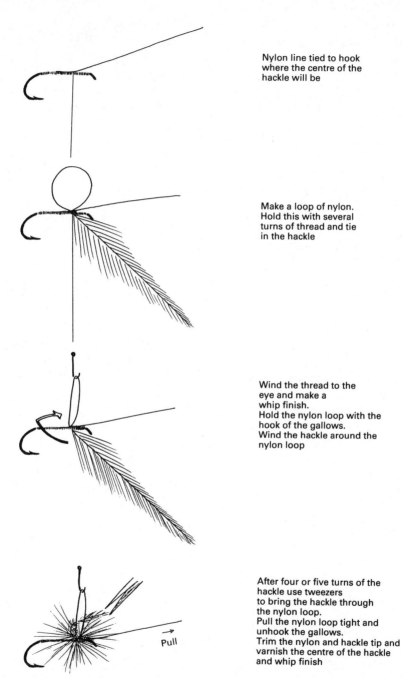

Nylon line tied to hook
where the centre of the
hackle will be

Make a loop of nylon.
Hold this with several
turns of thread and tie
in the hackle

Wind the thread to the
eye and make a
whip finish.
Hold the nylon loop with the
hook of the gallows.
Wind the hackle around the
nylon loop

After four or five turns of the
hackle use tweezers
to bring the hackle through
the nylon loop.
Pull the nylon loop tight and
unhook the gallows.
Trim the nylon and hackle tip and
varnish the centre of the hackle
and whip finish

Pull

Figure 10.8. Tying a parachute hackle.

To tie a parachute hackle, decide beforehand at which point on the shank the hackle has to be centred. As the thread is wound down the shank, tie in a piece of nylon line (about 4 lb breaking strain) so that the point at which the nylon is tied in will be the centre of the hackle. Continue winding the thread towards the tail, securing the nylon as you go and trimming it just before the tail is reached. The long end of the nylon is left projecting over the eye. Tie in the tail and body material and wind the thread back to where the nylon was fixed. Make a loop in the nylon and secure it with no more than two turns. Hook this loop onto the gallows and tie in the hackle by the stalk. Wind the thread on towards the eye. Wind the body material along the shank and past the nylon loop and hackle where it is finished as normal. Make a whip finish (see Figure 13.1) but do not varnish it yet. Take the tip of the hackle in the pliers and wind it around the base of the loop four or five times. Pass the hackle tip through the loop with the aid of tweezers and hold it firmly. Pull the long end of the nylon past the hook's eye which should secure the hackle point. Trim the scrap hackle point and place a very small drop of varnish in the centre of the hackle at this point and on the whip finish. The fly is complicated a little further if a pair of wings is added. Usually these are made of hair or hackle tips and are tied in before the body is wound on (Figure 10.8).

It is always important to make sure, no matter which feather is chosen, that the length of the fibre will match the proportions of the rest of the fly. Hackles never look as good if the tips of the fibres are cut into blunt stumps. Even if it looked well to trim all round a hackle, it is not easy to make it look presentable. There is, however, one occasion when trimming a hackle after tying might be considered. A dry fly with a bushy stiff hackle will often land unpredictably on the water. It may roll onto its side especially if the flue is too long. If the bottom hackle tips are snipped off in a straight line, level with the hook point, this may help ensure an upright position in the water.

11 Wings

General

What exactly is the purpose of an artificial fly's wing? The answer is not as simple as it might appear. When a natural dun, spinner, adult midge, sedge and so on is to be represented, the purpose is clearly to imply the presence of natural wings of the correct size and shape. This is certainly true of wings constructed of pieces of feather taken from a starling wing for example, even though they are not as translucent as the real thing.

A much more translucent means of tying such wings is to use one or two bunches of hackle fibre of the right shade, but these are not likely to produce the wing profile accurately. I have found such flies to be more successful than those with a more distinct profile.

Many of the naturals accepted by trout are likely to be damaged by waves and drowning which indicates that profile is not nearly so vital as past flytiers of the 'imitation' school believed. There is, too, a school of thought that claims that wings are unnecessary — hackle dry flies and traditional spider patterns are known to take fish when trout are feeding on the winged natural. Here the hackle not only implies legs and movement but the wings as well.

A black gnat (Plate 10) has flat wings over the top of its body, but fish feeding on these can often be taken on artificials with upward pointing wings or none at all. Usually the degree of imitation needed in a fly depends on how selectively the fish are feeding rather than on the structure of the natural insect or artificial fly.

The need for appropriate size and shade of wings, as with every other part of the fly, must be considered from two viewpoints: whether or not it is vital to the trout or the fisherman. I am quite sure that fish are seldom too fussy provided that the fly is presented well enough. If the angler is happy with the fly his presentation will invariably be better. The minutiae of the dressing may be blamed for failure when the angler is at fault.

The wings of a traditional winged wet fly may, when combined with the correct form and colour of the body, suggest some form of life but nothing too specific. Mallard and Claret is a fine example. A Tippet and Silver is a quite different proposition. Surely here the wings are merely one of a number of attractively combined materials.

Salmon fly wings mostly fall into the same category. The very elaborate dressings of the classic salmon flies seem to have evolved by a competition to get as many exotic materials included as possible, rather than practical angling effectiveness. Beautiful as they are no one can seriously claim that the inclusion of any one part of such a wing is significantly important in catching fish.

Providing the combined materials produce the desired tone what else is needed? The solid character of these wings is now considered by most anglers to be a disadvantage when compared with the more translucent quality of hair wings, which are much simpler to tie and very much more durable.

The relative merits of one form or one material will forever be a matter of debate, personal preference, or even prejudice. Hopefully, this will continue because absolute certainty in the attractive qualities of any fly or material would destroy much of the fun in angling. New materials are always being experimented with but who can say whether these materials make any contribution to attracting fish? Is it not the presentation of the fly by the angler which is the most critical factor?

Much of what follows may appear to be a little fussy. However, I have tried throughout to exclude anything which is not relevant to producing durable flies which do the job for which they are intended.

The standard feather wing of a wet or dry fly consists of two pieces of matched feather fibre. These are placed next to each other so that the natural bend in the feather either makes the pieces lie alongside each other without a gap — most common in wet flies — or set next to each other so that the feathers' natural curve separates the points of the wing pieces, most common on dry flies.

The feathers for this purpose are taken mostly from the wing or tail of the bird. Choosing the right feather for the job is vital, not only for appearance but also for ease of working. Points to watch for are:

1 The fibres of each feather must be in good condition without any hint of raggedness or splits.
2 The two pieces to be tied in must match one another in shade and markings as nearly as possible.
3 Each piece must have exactly the same number of fibres.
4 The natural curve of each piece must be the same on each piece.

Now we know what to look for in our feathers, how do we go about selecting them? With tail feathers, used for wet rather than dry flies, the problem is easy to solve, especially if the chosen feather is taken from the centre of the bird's tail; for example, the pheasant's centre tail used for the Invicta (Plate 11). On such feathers the length of the fibres on each side of the stalk and their natural curve should be identical and the markings should be almost identical.

Each piece may have to be taken from slightly different parts of the stalk in order to match the markings. But primary wing feathers (from starling for example), commonly used for wet and dry flies, are a different proposition. Only the fibres from one side of the stalk are used and even more care must be taken when choosing them.

First, make sure that the pair of wings to be used are from the same bird. All too often wings sold as pairs are not. I don't know why this should be except for a lack of care on the part of some dealers. It is surprising how unmatched wings from different birds of the same species can vary. This is important: ensuring a good match affects not only appearance but also makes tying easier. The best way of getting a real pair is to buy a complete skin.

Pick a feather from one wing and its twin from the other. Then decide which part of the feather to use for your construction. The shade and shape of a cut section of feather will change depending on its position.

Wet fly wings

Wet fly wings are simpler than the dry so here we will begin. Incidentally such wings may be tied before or after the hackle. With a false hackle the order is irrelevant but a collar hackle will make a difference. I prefer to tie in the wing after the hackle, except for some sedge patterns (Plate 7), as I find it easier and I think it looks better. No matter which style is required for wet or dry fly wings the number of fibres taken from each feather is important. They must be the same or the wing will develop a tilt when it is tied in. Err on the slim side. The fewer the fibres the easier and neater the wing will be, at least at first.

It always helps to use a fine pair of dividers when choosing which section of feather to use. It helps — but surprisingly is not always foolproof — in getting an equal number of fibres. Also, you will be able to judge if the two chosen sections have the same natural curve before cutting them out. They must be treated with the utmost care to avoid damage in the making. Leave that to the fish's teeth. Place the two sections together so they lie beside each other without a gap between them; i.e. place the tops of the feather sections together with their undersides outwards. Decide how the wing is to look for length: usually about the length of the body or a fraction longer. Then, do you wish the tips of the wing fibres to point upwards or down? I strongly prefer the upward pointing variety for purely aesthetic reasons.

Hold these pieces tightly together between the finger and thumb so the bottom fibres of the wing rest on the top of the hook shank at the desired spot. This is generally close to the eye leaving only enough room for the hackles and whip finish. The tying thread ought to be hanging vertically down below this point. Bring it over the top of the hook in a very loose turn and hold it firmly between finger and thumb with the wing. Holding the wing firmly, pull the thread straight down thus closing the loop down on the wing and clamping one fibre on top of the next until all are tight onto the hook. The wing sections must be held very tight during this operation. One or two turns in this fashion may be required to ensure the wing is well fixed before releasing it. Some flytiers advise that instead of securing the wing on the first downward pull of thread it should be given another loose half turn so that the pull to fix the wing is upward. I find this necessary only when a bulky wing is needed as it can prevent the wing from being pulled around the shank as the thread tightens. Trim off the scrap close to the hook and tie the head (Figure 11.1).

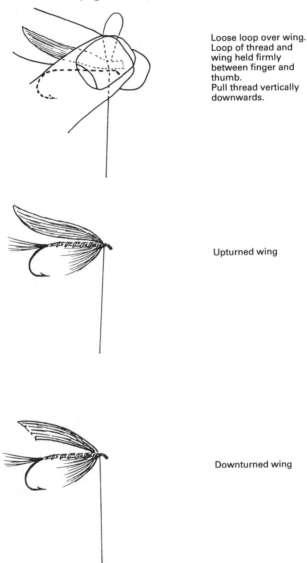

Loose loop over wing.
Loop of thread and wing held firmly between finger and thumb.
Pull thread vertically downwards.

Upturned wing

Downturned wing

Figure 11.1. Tying a wet fly wing.

Dry fly wings

Of all the methods of tying dry fly wings for duns only one has really
proved itself for me. It illustrates how one part of a fly may be used to
make another part more convincing. It is also one of the very few occasions
when a material can be successfully whipped to the shank without a layer
of thread beneath it.

Having chosen two pieces of sound primary wing fibre (as for wet flies),
place them both together with the tips level and the underneath parts of the
feather pieces back-to-back. This should ensure that the points will
naturally separate when held together by the cut ends. Both pieces must
now be tied together before fixing to the hook.

This is done by placing them in winging pliers so that the point at which
the wings are to be tied to the hook lies in the gap of the jaws. Make a loop
of thread around the feather pieces, tie a thumb knot with it and pull tight.
This draws all the fibres together to a fine point. Make a second thumb
knot to secure it. Remove the wing pieces from the pliers and trim the
thread very close to the feather. Cut away some of the scrap end with
scissors so that it tapers to a point. It is now ready for fixing to the hook.
Wing pliers are not really necessary. The same result is obtained if the wing
pieces are held between finger and thumb instead of winging pliers,
provided the pieces are gripped firmly as the knot is tightened.

Fixing to the hook should be done immediately after the thread is secure
on the hook at the beginning of tying. For this purpose begin to bind the
thread to the hook a little closer to the eye than usual. Hold the wing by the
scrap end over the hook so that the thread hangs below the point where the
wing pieces are to be tied.

The wing should point over the eye of the hook with the convex curve of
the wing uppermost. These wing pieces are tied in similarly to wet fly wings
after which the thread is taken in close even turns towards the tail over the
tapered scrap ends. This gives a good basis for the body and helps it to
taper towards the tail. After the body of the fly is finished the wings are
pulled to the required angle to the shank (usually 90 degrees) and set in
that position by a few turns of thread in front. Lastly, make sure that the
wings are sufficiently separated by gently pressing a dubbing needle down
between them. All that is needed to finish the fly is a hackle wound on
either side of the wings (Figure 11.2 and Plate 8).

All other wing types are either built as those described above or are very
simple.

Flytiers have, over the years, developed winged flies to suit their own
areas and techniques and every possible insect on the trout's menu. There
are long and short wings, split wings on wet flies and the standard wet fly
style used in dry sedges. Wings can be inclined from straight back towards

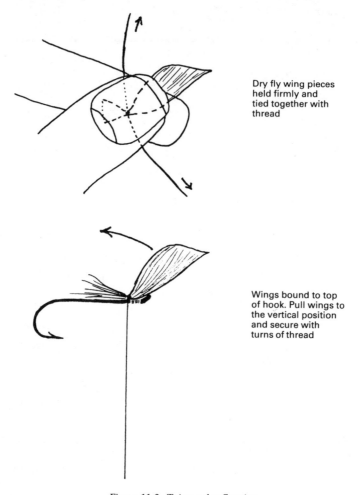

Dry fly wing pieces
held firmly and
tied together with
thread

Wings bound to top
of hook. Pull wings to
the vertical position
and secure with
turns of thread

Figure 11.2. Tying a dry fly wing.

the tail to over the eye and all points between. There are even wings to represent hatching, adult and dead (spent) insects.

It is always interesting to know the style designed for a particular type of water or area but it is wrong to treat these as though they were the only ones to use.

Emerging wings

Flies to represent hatching duns and midges can use wing materials identical to ordinary wet or dry ones. A Gold Ribbed Hare's Ear, for example, which implies a wide variety of hatching insects (especially the ephemeroptera or up-winged flies), can be tied wingless or have back-to-back split wings or even a bunch of hackle fibres or hair (Plate 8) depending on preference. Other emergers, such as the Duck fly (Plate 6) intended to represent a hatching midge, have a different method. Each piece of feather is, in turn, placed alongside the body of the fly and tied so that the fibres of each, at the point of tying in, form a semi-circle around one side of the shank. It takes practise to manage this without all the fibres separating, but it is worth taking the trouble for appearances sake. Neatness, however, does not make the fly any more effective. Preparing each piece as though it were a dry fly wing or using hackle points or hackle fibres also works well.

A section of goose biot when trimmed to shape can be used for the more modern patterns of hatching midge (Figure 11.3).

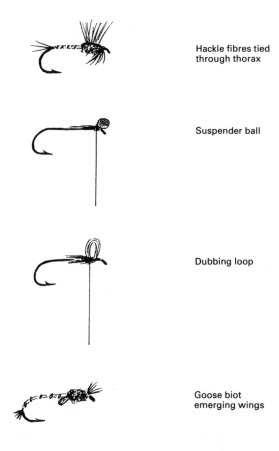

Hackle fibres tied
through thorax

Suspender ball

Dubbing loop

Goose biot
emerging wings

Figure 11.3. Various types of emerging wings.

For some hatching flies, particularly those which represent up-winged flies a bunch of hackle fibres may be used to represent emerging wings by tying the bunch in the middle of the nymph thorax so that they point vertically upwards. The wing cases, which are usually made of feather fibre, are then pulled over the thorax on either side of the emerging wings (Figure 11.3). A bunch of such fibres tied on top of an adult midge body is an easy and very effective winging method which can be adapted for a variety of other flies too.

Yet another method is simply to tie in a small bunch of dubbing fur of the correct shape. Modern synthetic dubbing with long fibres is ideal for this. Some patterns even call for a loop of dubbing fur which is intended to do the same job. However, this has serious durability problems (Figure 11.3).

A method which has a dual-purpose representation and flotation utilises a small bead of polystyrene or ethafoam covered with stocking material. This is then tied in near the eye of the hook by the fabric. The result is a 'suspender nymph' which can be coloured using an indelible felt-tip pen (Figure 11.3).

Folded or rolled wings

Folded or rolled feather wings are perhaps not so neat or sharp in profile but they are very easy to tie and they have the significant advantage of being more durable than other winging methods. They may be totally opaque which is a quality used to good effect on flies such as the Kingsmill.

A wing made of bronze mallard, mallard grey flank or teal is most easily constructed by folding or rolling the feather and is more translucent. Cut a section of feather and fold it twice keeping the outside of the feather visible and tie it in as described earlier. This produces the best results with small bunches of fibre provided that the natural curve of the feather is ironed out by drawing the fibres away from the stalk with thumb and forefinger before cutting the fibres. This also ensures that the tips of the fibres are level (Plate 3).

For teal wing flies I like to use this method on the larger versions but on small ones I simply use a bunch of fibres cut or torn from the feather, as on the Peter Ross (Plate 11). Such a method will not win prizes but it is quick and very effective. The 'proper' way to make a teal wing is to take a small breast feather and fold it over along the stalk and press it together. When it has been pressed for long enough to retain this upturned boat shape it is tied in by the stalk. That is the theory which I find is surprisingly time consuming and ineffective. It is very difficult to make the feather keep its set; I have resorted to spraying with starch and pressing with a steam iron without reasonable results. Maybe it is just my fault.

Not having the exact shade of feather which is required for a particular fly need not stop you from making an effective fly. If one feather does not have exactly the right shade it is a simple matter to take several fibres from different feathers and roll or bunch them together. This is not often used but is, perhaps, worth a try. It is a method more common for hair wings, but why not employ it for feathers when appropriate or if you do not have a single feather of the desired shade?

Married fibre wings

Married fibre wings can look stunning but I am quite sure that they are irrelevant as far as the fish are concerned. They are the sort of thing to try only as a test of skill after you have all the practical flies you need. It is vital to use the right sort of feather for some will work much better than others. I have found that goose shoulder feathers are the easiest to marry but swan shoulder, turkey tail and a few others can be used. Normally, only join feathers of the same texture; for example, goose to goose. If you try to join goose shoulder to coarser turkey tail you will find that the hooks on each side of the feather fibres will not interlock properly. If two different types of feather must be joined (say, turkey to swan) try to make sure that the fibres are of the same thickness and/or texture.

To marry pieces of feather, simply place them together edge-to-edge and stroke them gently between finger and thumb. The result should look like one piece of feather with different stripes of colour rather than different pieces of feather (see front cover). Three married colours is usually enough for any fly, but make sure of two things in the making:

1   Remember when taking pieces of feather that the final married section will be two or three times wider, so err on the narrow side for each colour.
2   Be careful to watch the natural curve of the pieces to be married or they will not sit right on the fly and soon become 'divorced'.

Hackle point wings

There is a wide variety of applications for hackle point wings on representative trout flies and lures, and even some salmon flies. Both cock and hen hackle points may be used in their natural form. Hen hackles are more often shaped beforehand. The main difficulty with tying them is to make sure they do not twist out of position as the thread is tightened.

For spent spinners, take two small cock hackles of the correct size and strip away the scrap fibres at the base. Take each feather in turn, after the body has been finished, and set it on top of the shank so that it is at right angles to it. Make one turn of thread around the shank and across the stalk and repeat this in the opposite direction. Care must be taken to ensure that the wings are the same length and that they have not been twisted out of the horizontal plane by the thread. When this is done one or two more figure of eight turns, as before, should secure the wings before the scrap ends of the stalks are trimmed away. The hackle is then wound either side of the wings in the same fashion. I sometimes use one or two variations on this. The first turn around the stalk is not needed if the hackle tip is secured to the top of the hook in the correct manner (see Figure 4.1).

With large hackle tips it is occasionally advisable to tie them in right at the beginning so that the stalks may be bent round to lie alongside the shank, the body dressing on top helping to keep them more secure.

One point to bear in mind for this type of wing, is to make sure that when the hackle point is tied in there should be a short length of fibreless stalk showing. This is important, to ensure that when the hackle is wound the fibres of the wing are not forced out of place.

A similar wing effect is obtained by winding a hackle around the shank, separating the left and right sides into two bunches and then holding them in this position by several figure of eight turns. This can be bulky but can simulate the thorax well (Figure 11.4).

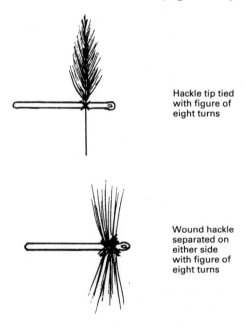

Hackle tip tied
with figure of
eight turns

Wound hackle
separated on
either side
with figure of
eight turns

Figure 11.4. Tying spent wings.

A pair of Daddy Long Legs wings can be tied similarly but, because these wings are so large, the chance of breaking them during a cast is greatly increased; air resistance when casting these flies may also cause difficulties. Usually the wings are tied in so as to sweep backwards over the top of the body (Plate 10). With a dapping version of this fly the problem does not arise.

Adult midges and the diptera, or flat wing, family require a similar form. I have found the best way to do this is to hold the hackle points in turn, pointing backwards on the top of the hook. A turn or two should be enough to hold each. The wings should be separated slightly, either by one figure of eight turn or simply by hand. The hackle is wound in front of the wings but not between them.

Shaped and whole feather wings

When hen hackle points are used on representational flies it is usual to shape them first, either by use of a wing cutter or by gripping the feather in wing formers and burning off the tips of the fibres. I much prefer the cutters. If used for flat winged flies, such as midges, cow dung flies and gnats, the method is identical to that already described. For the up-winged or ephemeroptera variety this type of wing can be formed in two ways: one, by cutting a hen hackle or similar feather to shape, or two, by using whole Mallard breast feathers to form the fan wings which are most commonly seen on Mayfly patterns (Plate 10).

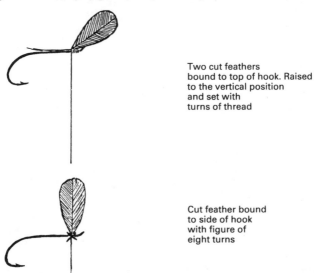

Two cut feathers
bound to top of hook. Raised
to the vertical position
and set with
turns of thread

Cut feather bound
to side of hook
with figure of
eight turns

Figure 11.5. Tying a shaped feather wing.

One method of tying this type of wing is to hold the feathers along the shank so that the wings extend over the eye of the hook. The stalks are then bound together on top of the hook. This is often best done as the first tying operation. When the body has been finished the wings are gripped between finger and thumb and held in the vertical position where a few turns of thread will secure the correct set. If required, these wing feathers can be split and held apart with figure of eight turns of thread.

Another method is to hold each feather in turn so that the stalk runs vertically downwards on one side of the shank. A figure of eight should hold it while this is repeated on the other side. The wings are now in the correct position with the stalk extending below the hook. Draw both stalks together up to the underside of the hook and bind them down along it. Then tie the rest of the fly. This is identical to the midge wing method except that the figure of eight turns are in a different plane (Figure 11.5).

Mutuka wings

Matukas are, like the Muddler series, popular and especially favoured on stillwater. I don't know why their shape should be more attractive than a host of other lures but they certainly work. What interests us here is the method of tying which makes them distinctive.

The tying of a Matuka begins, as for any other artificial, to the point where the body material (often chenille) and rib is tied in at the bend. Wind on the body but not the rib. At this point take two hen hackles of the right colour and remove two thirds of the fibres from one side of each. Place both feathers back-to-back with the stripped sides, along the top of the body, and tie the stalks in at the head. Draw the top fibres to a vertical position and wind the rib, usually of oval, evenly to the head through the fibres on top where the rib and hen hackle wings are secured with tying thread. Then trim off the scrap and make the head (Figure 11.6).

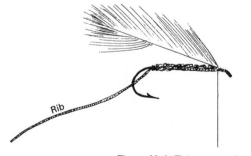

Two hen hackles tied in at the eye and bound to the top of the body with turns of ribbing

Rib

Figure 11.6. Tying a matuka.

A similar method is used to tie in a narrow strip of rabbit fur on the skin to make Zonkers and similar flies. In such flies the rabbit skin may appear rather bulky when it is being tied but its mobility in the water more than compensates for this.

Synthetic wings

Polythene, clear or dyed, is an excellently realistic method of suggesting wings provided the right type is chosen to suit the required fly. The polythene should not be too flimsy for reasons of durability but if it is too thick it becomes difficult to tie in neatly and firmly. The resealable bags in which many materials are sold are usually ideal. There are specially veined synthetic sheets available in a variety of textures and shades intended to represent the wings of many insects. They can look well but are expensive and is a fish going to notice? I have experimented with other materials such as flectolite — the results were interesting but that is all.

First, fold the polythene and press it flat. Press the cutter so that the ends of the blade just reach beyond the fold in the polythene. The wings should then open out showing a very narrow strip of polythene between the two ends.

If spent wings are required simply set the wings on top of the hook with the narrowest part of the polythene on the shank and secure them with several figure of eight turns.

For flatwing flies I have found the best way is to start as the above and draw each wing back over the top of the body where its set is held by a few turns of thread. It helps to keep the polythene between the wings as narrow as possible, to avoid untidy and bulky dressing. It is possible to pull the wings apart and tie them in separately, but since polythene is such a slippery material the figure of eight gives extra strength (Figure 11.7).

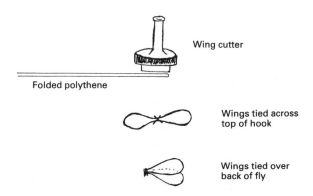

Figure 11.7. Cutting synthetic wings.

Hair wings

As the fashion for using hair as a wing material really took hold for salmon flies more and more materials of differing lengths, stiffness and texture have become available, so that hair is now appearing in all manner of fly wings and is extremely successful.

The most important qualities of hair are its translucency and mobility. This is the key to its success, but as with all other aspects of fly dressing economy is vital. The less material that is used, up to a point, the better the impression of translucency and the more mobility which probably leads to greater success.

Not least among hair's virtues is its ease of tying. However, there is one problem which many beginners encounter with hair wings and that is the fibres falling out of the finished fly. The turns of thread become loose and the fly disintegrates. There can be two reasons for this: using too much hair, which is the most common problem; or, the fibres being naturally slippery, squirrel for example. Using less material will solve both problems easily, so even if a large wing is needed several bunches will be held better than one large bunch. No matter how small a bunch is used, a small drop of superglue on the tied-in ends makes a very secure wing. It is very important to make the most appropriate choice of wing hair as far as mobility is concerned. Fibres from various sources can have widely differing qualities as the following examples illustrate:

Bucktail	Long fibres which are stiff, coarse, almost straight and of every colour.
Grey Squirrel	Medium length, soft, fine, straight, black bars unless bleached.
Calf Tail	Short, medium stiffness, kinked, of every colour.
Hackle Fibre	Short, fine, straight, all colours.

Naturally, the larger the fibres the more movement they will have, but I have found in most cases squirrel and hackle fibres to be the most mobile and calf tail the least. When the scrap ends are being removed, always cut at an angle across the fibres. This will stop a lump from forming over which the tying thread can slip (Figure 11.8).

Not only are there many possibilities from the above list as it stands but there are ways to widen its scope. Hair from different sources may be blended with interesting results, but it is a good idea not to combine the coarsest and finest in the interests of solid construction. Shortening fibres may decrease their mobility, the extent to which any natural curve may influence the fly and colour combination achieved. If buoyancy is an important feature of the fly, deer hair may be used, but it is very coarse and does not take dye very well.

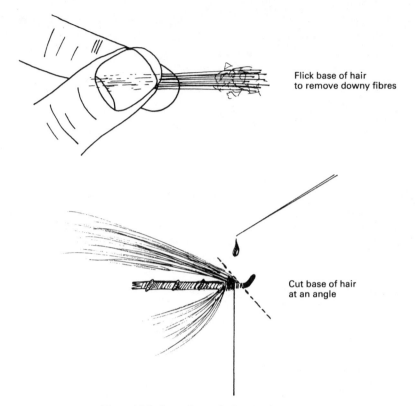

Flick base of hair
to remove downy fibres

Cut base of hair
at an angle

Figure 11.8. Preparing and trimming hair wings.

More and more hair wings are employed in the representation of naturals and other trout flies. They can make very effective flies, but it would be a great pity if other forms were totally forgotten. There are too few tiers capable of the more complex traditional methods as it is.

For the wings of a dun or spinner simply tie a bunch of hair to the shank with the tips of the hair over the hook eye and use a few turns in front or behind the bunch to obtain the correct set of wing. If required a few figure of eight turns of thread will split the bunch evenly.

On some sedge flies a bunch of fibres is tied in before the hackle, in the same way as for a hair wing wet fly. This is one of the few occasions when chopping the tips off the fibres may improve the sedge fly profile, if this is done just beyond the bend of the hook, as on Richard Walker's patterns.

Hair is an increasingly popular material for wet fly wings on trout as well as salmon flies. It may be difficult to obtain hair which matches the shade of starling wing quills or bronze mallard so common on loch flies. However, it could be argued that in most, if not all, cases an exact match is quite unnecessary. What a fly may lose in shade it more than makes up for in translucency and movement. There is a parallel here with my method of exchanging wet fly wings for hackles, but hair wings may roughly maintain the traditional profile.

Many tiers suggest that hair wings must be tamped before tying. This means placing the hairs in a tube points downwards and tapping the tube to ensure that all the tips of the hairs are level. I seldom bother wasting too much time on this unless the hairs are of widely differing lengths. This results in a less distinct wing profile which is the reason for using hair in the first place (Plates 13 and 14).

Much more important is to grip the hairs near the tips and flick the blunt ends to remove the fluffy fibres which only serve to add bulk to the tying. Modern winging materials such as marabou, Lureflash and a wide range of other synethetic materials are becoming more popular. They were originally used mainly for rainbow trout lures but are now used for a wide variety of fly types, either on their own or blended with natural hair. Some synthetic materials are expensive so it is important to assess their value critically. It is impossible to be sure whether or not the inclusion of one of these flashy materials is responsible for success or failure in a fly. In some situations the novelty value is more important than any imagined quality of the material, but they are now so popular that many people will disagree.

There are also those people who argue that such materials are too gaudy and may in some circumstances be counter productive. You pay your money and take your chance.

Built wings

Built wings of mixed feathers are called for by the inventors of the old-style salmon flies, but not by the fish. Most modern authorities on the subject claim that such flies succeed, in spite rather than because of the dressing, and few now would argue.

In my opinion, however, dressing is still worth the effort, for two reasons: one, the degree of difficulty as a test of skill ensures that the skills of the Victorian fly dressers do not die altogether; and, two, simply because of their beauty. Flytying is only a means to the end of catching fish. Virtually any concoction can do that at least some of the time. But for most modern flytiers these flies are for display only. They are impractical and this is compounded by the expense of materials and the difficulty of obtaining them. They are worth a try if only for their looks. The following few notes might be of use in pursuing this.

The procedure is very similar to tying in ordinary feather wings, except that several separate tyings are required as close together as possible. It is this which causes the problems with this type of wing. To overcome such difficulties is easy in theory but requires some practice to perfect.

First, the choice of materials is important: materials must be as fine as possible. For example, never use goose or swan wing feathers; the shoulders are much more suitable in terms of their bulk and willingness to be shaped by the fingers to obtain the correct set. As with other wings, always use as little material as you can, at first anyway. Have all the materials required prepared and ready before you start, it is this which takes more time than the actual tying. A typical wing contains: an underwing of turkey tail or tippet feather; several strips of married fibre from goose or swan; strips of bronze mallard, bustard and golden pheasant tail which may be married or even folded over the top of the previous wing section; and a topping of golden pheasant crest.

So there are four tyings needed to produce the basic salmon fly wing. Take the two pieces of turkey, from either side of a single tail feather, place them back-to-back and tie them in, in exactly the same manner as a normal feather wet fly wing. This should be done immediately after the throat or collar hackle has been applied.

As for the set of the wings this is a matter of choice but it is traditional to tie the first component of the wing lying close to the body. This is achieved by bending the pieces of turkey at their base so that the fibres slip over each other a little. Four close tight turns are made to hold the wing and the scrap removed. Golden pheasant tippet feathers may also be used to form the underwing, either whole or trimmed when a very slim wing is required.

An alternative, and very successful, means of obtaining the required set for the wing is to prepare the thread foundation on which the wing is to be tied. Regardless of the type of wing to be tied the foundation must be smooth and constructed with turns of well-waxed thread.

If the required set of the wing is along the body the foundation may be built up in order to slope down and away from the eye of the hook. This technique is useful for some salmon flies and the wings of sedges.

Alternatively, if the wing is to be set at a steep angle to the hook shank (appropriate to many wet trout flies especially those which represent the up-winged flies), a similar foundation can be created but sloping downwards towards the eye (Figure 11.9).

When you are ready with the married fibre unwind the last two turns, which should give a tiny flat platform on which to tie this second part. Again, four turns secure it; unwind two before the next piece is tied in. This third piece is different in that it overlaps the married fibre a little. A very simple way to do this is to take a section of bronze mallard, for example, and fold it over the already secure wing and tie it in, in the usual way.

The final element of many salmon fly wings and even some traditional

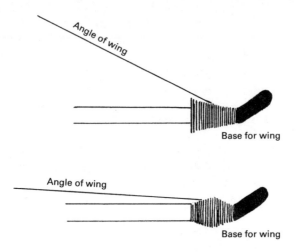

Figure 11.9. Preparing the foundation of a wing.

trout and sea trout dressings is a topping, generally taken from the crest of a golden pheasant. This feather is usually tied in its natural golden yellow but may be dyed red for some patterns.

The topping, in conjunction with the same material used as a tail, should form a golden frame or halo to the wing. Therefore the tips of both these feathers should touch each other without overlapping. Tying in the topping is a slightly more difficult task than it may at first appear. Few crest feathers can be tied in straight from the bird in a way which either looks neat or fulfils the function of creating a halo. These feathers need to be moulded to shape. This process takes time and should not be left until the feather is required.

Ideally the size and shape of the wing should be decided a few hours at least before beginning to tie the fly (Figure 11.10). Simple outlines can be placed under a piece of clear perspex or glass. The chosen tail and topping feathers are then wetted, placed over the outline and shaped to match it. When dry the feathers ought to maintain the chosen shape. If you intend to tie large numbers of such flies it clearly makes sense to make up these tails and toppings in bulk and store them carefully.

Even when all this has been completed there is one last operation which is required before tying. Grip the tip of the crest feather with your left hand, then squeeze the tying point of the feather vertically between the thumbnail and finger tip of your right hand. This should flatten the stalk of the feather sufficiently to avoid the feather twisting as it is tied in (Figure 11.10).

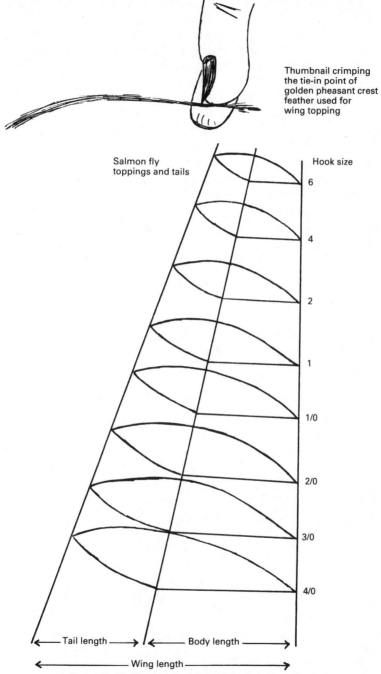

Thumbnail crimping the tie-in point of golden pheasant crest feather used for wing topping

Salmon fly toppings and tails

Hook size

6

4

2

1

1/0

2/0

3/0

4/0

Tail length

Body length

Wing length

Figure 11.10. Shaping the tail topping of a salmon fly.

Sides and cheeks

Sides and cheeks are tied along either side of a fly's wing. Most often they are found on fully-dressed salmon flies but may also feature on a small range of trout flies such as the Alexandra or Kingsmill. Even some modern lure patterns employ cheeks; for example, the Hanningfield Lure.

The only distinction between sides and cheeks is their length. Sides tend to extend about one half to two-thirds of the length of the wing, whereas cheeks are shorter at about one-third of the length of the wing. In most cases their purpose is purely decorative but perhaps the enamel-like dots of the jungle cock may suggest the eyes of small fish on some patterns.

Some tiers may find that the addition of a cheek is a quick and simple method of hiding imperfections in the tying of wings and hackles.

It is a very simple matter to place the chosen cheek or side feathers on either side of the wing and secure them with a few turns of thread. Care needs to be taken, though, to ensure that both sides are the same length; so, before finishing the fly, look vertically downwards on it and adjust the side accordingly.

Occasionally, the feathers when tied in will tend to stick out like fins on either side of the wing. This should not happen if the base is properly prepared. Before tying the cheeks simply make a few turns of thread towards the eye of the hook and back again, thus covering all the scrap pieces of feather from wings and hackles which have caused the problem. The sides or cheeks should now hug the sides of the wings when tied in (Figure 11.11).

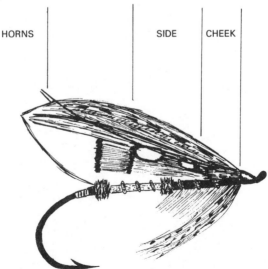

HORNS   SIDE   CHEEK

Figure 11.11. Finished traditional salmon fly showing proportion of wings

12 Horns and Antennae

Horns are a superfluous addition to some salmon fly wings, but antennae often appear on representations of naturals such as sedges in an attempt to make them look more realistic.

The reason for grouping horns and antennae together here, despite antennae not being part of any wing, is that each consists of two fibres (feather or hair) tied in similarly. The only practical difference between horns and antennae is the direction in which they point.

Horns on a fully dressed salmon fly seem to be there for the same reason as much of the rest of the wing, decoration only. Not surprisingly their omission does not seem to adversely affect the performance of these flies. Normally, only one type of feather is used, macaw. These are blue on top and red or yellow underneath. Simply tie one fibre on each side of the wing to run alongside the main wing. The natural curve of each fibre can be made to point slightly upwards or downwards according to preference.

Antennae point over the eye to represent the real thing on a sedge adult or over the body for pupae such as longhorns (Plate 7). Either feather fibre or hair can be used. Choice of material does not matter too much for the adult because they are fairly short, about body length. The pupae can have antennae which are very much longer.

No matter which material you pick there will be durability problems; for example, both soft and stiff fibres will break easily. Use horse or goat hair to offset this, both work reasonably well. It is, also, preferable on adult sedge patterns to tie in the antennae at the beginning, finish the rest of the dressing over the blunt ends and secure the correct 'V'-shaped set with several turns at the end. Alternatively, tying the antennae in last on pupae is easier (Plate 12.1).

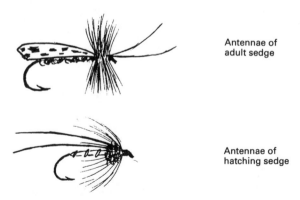

Antennae of
adult sedge

Antennae of
hatching sedge

Figure 12.1. Tying in the antennae.

13 Heads

To form an artificial fly's head three functions may need to be taken into account — though not all flies will necessarily require all three. First, make a whip finish. This will only require four turns of thread, and may be enough for some flies. Second, on a large number of patterns the scrap ends of hackles and wings must be covered with a few tight turns of thread. Third, a relatively small number of patterns require the head to be built up into a pronounced feature with tying thread, herl, deer hair, bead or a variety of other materials.

As we saw in making bodies (see Figure 9.1) a space must be left for the head. The size of this space will depend on which of the above three functions you require. Clearly the second and third require increasing room. Knowing how much space to allow for the head requires experience. You can usually get away with unusual lengths of wing or hackle without the fly losing all sense of proportion, but the wrong head size can detract from its aesthetic quality, despite being irrelevant in terms of catching fish in almost every case.

Beginners tend to leave too little room at first so that the head partly obscures the eye of the hook. The natural reaction to this is to over-compensate and allow far too much room before finally getting it right.

Generally speaking, the larger the fly the larger the head, particularly on built-wing salmon flies, for the simple reason that there is a lot of material which needs to be secured. However, on nearly all flies the size of the head can be reduced by using a drop of glue or varnish on the scrap ends and forming the head with turns of thread while this is still wet. Then the scrap ends can be cut very short.

There are two ways to do a whip finish, by hand or with a special tool designed for the job. Using the tool is the quickest and easiest method requiring very little practice (Figure 13.1). There are, however, several

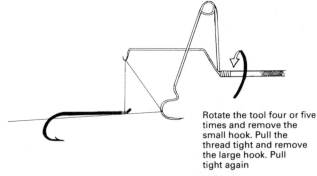

Rotate the tool four or five times and remove the small hook. Pull the thread tight and remove the large hook. Pull tight again

Figure 13.1. A whip finish

types of whip finish tool and although they all work you will probably find that those with large hooks are easier. No matter which style of whip finish tool is chosen it will not be suitable for all occasions. Finishing the body on the tail hook of a tandem mount is just one of several examples of this. In such cases the hand method is required where the fingers of the right hand take over from the hooks.

No matter which method is used to do a whip finish only about four turns of thread are needed provided the thread is waxed. The thread is then trimmed as close to the hook as possible; if your scissors are either too big or blunt a small piece of thread will be left which will become stiff and rough when the head is varnished. So, try to avoid this by using nail clippers instead of scissors.

The only fly which does not end with a whip finish is the parachute (see Figure 10.8).

Some flies require heads which are unusually large in comparison to the hook. The heads of some nymphs, the corixa (Plate 5), and several others have heads built up with turns of tying thread which are then varnished several times to cement the thread and to form a glossy head. There is a little more to such a head than simply making a lot of turns. They must be even. Uneven turns of thread on a large head can all too easily work loose and slip off towards the eye; this will also present a smooth finish when the head is varnished.

Many other materials may be built up into heads using herl, as in the Jersey Herd (Plate 12), or using deer hair as with Muddlers of various types (Plate 11). Shot also can be used, as with Leadheads.

A novel way to produce a pronounced and perfectly formed head which may also add weight is simply to thread a bead onto the hook before placing it in the vice. When the fly is complete the dressing should hold the bead tight to the eye and the whip finish is tied on the bend side of the bead. A little superglue may be added for insurance but it is not vital (Figure 13.2). I first saw this method being used to great effect in Holland,

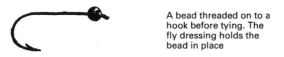

A bead threaded on to a hook before tying. The fly dressing holds the bead in place

Figure 13.2. Threading a bead.

at Fly Fair '90, where 'Goldheads' were being made. The beads in this case were of brass so the fly is fished with a sink and draw and behaves in the same way as a Dog Nobbler.

When the thread is tied off it must always be coated with varnish to cement the whipping. This may take the form of tiny drops applied with the point of a sharp needle. The varnish must always be as thin as possible otherwise it will not soak into the thread properly. When the head must be a large feature it may be coloured black, red or a variety of other colours. This is done either with varnish of the desired colour or thread of the correct colour coated in clear varnish, the former method being most appropriate for salmon flies and the latter for trout flies. In all cases, the larger the head the more coats of varnish required.

14 Eyes

As with all other aspects of artificial flies, eyes may be realistic, exaggerated or impressionistic. They may, too, be a means of adding weight to the fly near the eye of the hook, so that it will dive quickly and be made to rise in the water with every pull of the retrieve which seems to trigger the taking response in the fish. Alternatively, buoyant eyes such as on the Booby will float, or at least fish, higher in the water than a fast sinking line. With this fly every pull of the retrieve will make the fly sink — when the retrieve stops the fly rises. In each case a zig-zag motion is created, but by different means.

Bead chain eyes have become very popular on flies such as the Cat's Whisker (Plate 12). To make them, simply nip off two beads from a sink plug chain with cutting pliers. Then set them on the shank and bind them to the hook with figure of eight turns. A drop of glue on the binding will prevent the eyes slipping around the hook (Figure 14.1).

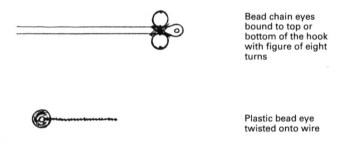

Bead chain eyes bound to top or bottom of the hook with figure of eight turns

Plastic bead eye twisted onto wire

Figure 14.1. Bead eyes.

Small plastic beads obtained from a craft shop are ideal for eye making and have the added advantage of offering a wide variety of colours. I have found the best way to fix such beads is to thread a double thickness of copper wire through a bead and twist the ends around each other, repeating this for the other eye. The twists of wire help grip when they are bound to the hook. The only disadvantage is the possibility of the wire breaking after prolonged use (Plate 15).

On very small flies the two techniques described above will rarely do. It is either difficult to obtain beads small enough or the twists of wire result in an unrealistically fat body. If eyes are required without additional weight there are a wide variety of possibilities.

Take two short lengths of nylon line and melt one end of each with a candle flame. The result should be a shiny black lump the size of which depends on the thickness of the nylon and the amount which is melted.

Practice is required to obtain two which are identical. It is a good idea to crimp the stalks of the eyes with pliers in order to roughen the surface which helps grip when they are tied in (Figure 14.2).

A similar result is achieved in a slightly different way. Melt one end of a piece of nylon as before then hold the nylon close to the eye with tweezers and melt the other end of the nylon to form the second eye. This is then placed on the hook and bound with figure of eight turns of thread (Figure 14.2).

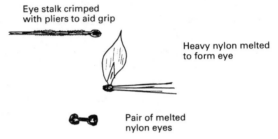

Figure 14.2. Forming nylon eyes.

Golden pheasant tippet feathers look nothing like real eyes but can be made to give the impression of eyes on the General Practitioner (Plate 15). Take a whole tippet feather, remove the poor quality fibres near the base of the stalk, and snip the stalk to remove the central short fibres. The remaining feather is then tied in flat over the top of the hook. The black tips of the feather should be roughly in line with the bend of the hook (Figure 14.3).

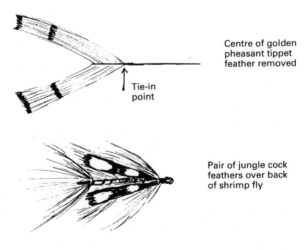

Figure 14.3. Eyes for salmon shrimps and prawns.

Two small bunches of tippet feather can be used to produce the same effect if they are tied in on either side of the shank. It is difficult to keep all the black tips level.

Jungle cock neck feathers are unique, with creamy white enamel-like dots which are opaque and reflective. They are only legally obtainable from birds bred in the United Kingdom and so are very expensive. They are used on a wide variety of flies as cheeks and may also represent the eyes or gills of a small fish. My most common use of these feathers is on traditional-style salmon shrimps (Plates 15 and 16). Whether or not these feathers actually do suggest a real shrimp's eyes seems very doubtful to me, however, there are basically two methods of tying them.

First, place two feathers back-to-back and tie them in like a wing before the final hackle. Or, second, and the one I prefer because it is easier to tie and the wings keep their set, wait until the final hackle of the shrimp is tied, then tie in each feather in turn over the back at a slight angle to the shank.

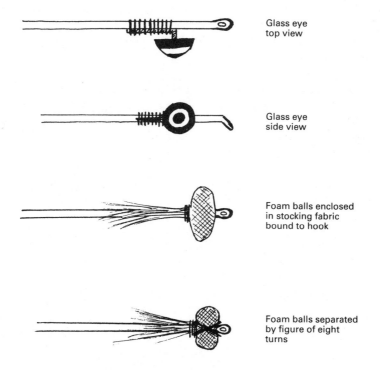

Glass eye
top view

Glass eye
side view

Foam balls enclosed
in stocking fabric
bound to hook

Foam balls separated
by figure of eight
turns

Figure 14.4. Doll eyes and boobies.

After both feathers are in position and held with a few turns of thread bend the stalks back on themselves and bind them down again. This adds virtually no bulk to the head but ensures that there is no possibility of the feathers being pulled out. They are too valuable to risk that (Figure 14.3).

Almost any feather which has dots can be used to suggest eyes — Sand grouse, Barn owl and Guinea fowl all have this property. Sometimes small slips of any white feather can be used for cheeks as a substitute for Jungle cock. I find this preferable to commercially produced Jungle cock substitute — black hen hackle with two blobs of paint — which is both coarse and hideous.

Paint, stamped rather than brushed, onto a well-varnished head can look alright but it is time consuming and almost certainly has no functional advantage. To stamp the paint on I prefer to use the end of a salmon tube, lightly dipped in white or silver paint; this produces a ring on the black head of Leadheads and some nymphs.

Some tiers make use of glass eyes on wire stems, of the kind used in making dolls. The wire is bent at right angles and nipped to the required length and bound to the hook. It is vital to glue this binding to prevent the eyes twisting on the hook. Eyes of this kind add weight to the fly which can occasionally be useful but are easily broken and consequently are rarely used (Figure 14.4).

The large bulging 'eyes' of a Booby fly add buoyancy and are tied in much the same way as the ball of a suspender nymph. To tie a Booby, two polystyrene or ethafoam balls are enclosed in stocking material and, when this is bound to the hook, figure of eight turns are used to separate the eyes, the result being a grotesque but effective fly.

15 Backs and Wing Cases

Here we are again concerned with the representation of parts of creatures on which fish feed and which may be reproduced using a vast range of materials.

The backs of beetles, freshwater shrimps, prawns and some fry patterns (Plates 9 and 15) have backs which extend for the whole length of the body and they may also have a rib over it. The wing cases of nymphs generally cover one half to one third of the back (Plates 8 and 9).

The older patterns almost exclusively make use of feather fibre such as cock pheasant tail. Generally speaking, these patterns are capable of producing the desired profile of any back but they are dull and unreflective, which is a problem with, for example, the Corixa (Plate 5), and other patterns.

Magpie feather is more reflective but there are better materials. Polythene and latex, dyed or plain, Spectraflash, Lureflash, etc. offer more possibilities. Freshwater shrimps (Plate 9) with a back of polythene over-ribbed with wire represent well the reflective segmented back of the natural. Latex has similar qualities, most commonly seen on salmon prawns.

Raffiene is both cheap and available in a wide range of colours. The backs of Corixa, Chompers and Polystickles are where it is most often seen. It must always be wet when tying so that when it is pulled over the back it will stretch smooth and be much more effective than if used dry.

If the backing material is to cover the whole length of the body it is tied in at or a little round the bend of the hook. After the remainder of the fly is tied the material is drawn tightly over the back of the fly and tied in at the head. The width of the material is important. The wider it is the more of the side of the body it will cover, which is important on many Freshwater Shrimp patterns (Plate 9). On such patterns it is useful to wind the ribbing after the back is tied in (Figure 15.1).

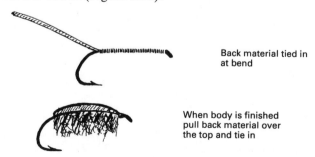

Back material tied in at bend

When body is finished pull back material over the top and tie in

Figure 15.1. Tying a back.

For the wing cases of an ephemeroptera nymph (Plate 8), for example, only the front part of the body is backed. It can be done in the same way as the full back, but there is another method. The abdomen of a nymph should become a little thicker from the tail to the thorax. This can be built up with a layer or two of thread but a better way could be to use the wing case material itself. Tie in the latter about one third of the way from the eye to the bend and bind the tapered scrap end to the hook as the thread is wound to the tail. Make the tail and abdomen of the nymph, pull the back material towards the tail, form the thorax and then tie in the wing case over the top (Figure 15.2).

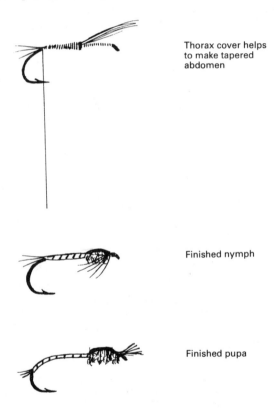

Thorax cover helps to make tapered abdomen

Finished nymph

Finished pupa

Figure 15.2. Tying in the wing case.

In each of the cases above some of the back material may be left extending over the eye of the hook, or pulled back to give the appearance of legs, without winding a hackle (Figure 15.2). This is used on Walker's Mayfly nymph (Plate 9).

A very popular style of dry fly in the United States uses a back of deer hair, not just for a back but also to aid flotation. Such flies are called Goofus Bugs or Humpies. This method is useful also because the ends of the deer hair may also be used to represent tails, wings and even legs. The result is a fly which is both functional and very quick to tie.

Fry patterns may use deer hair in a similar way to produce head, back and tail all in one. More often the back material of a fry pattern, such as Jersey Herd or Pearlstickle (Plates 9 and 12), forms the back and tail together. The material is simply allowed to extend beyond the body and trimmed to form a fish-like tail. Lureflash, raffiene, plastic sheet, flexibody and even the old fashioned feather fibre may all be used for this (Figure 15.3).

Simple fry pattern with tail material continued over the back

Figure 15.3. Back and tail of a fry pattern.

On realistic prawn patterns (Plate 15) Flexibody or heavy plastic sheet is the best choice. It is durable as well as looking the part. To add a touch of realism I make two turns of ribbing then pull the back over and tie it in followed by three turns of ribbing over everything. A small piece of back material is left over the hook eye for the same reason (Figure 15.4). Prawn patterns of a more impressionistic nature also have backs. The golden pheasant breast feathers tied in flat over the top of the body are intended to fulfil this function on a General Practitioner (Plate 15).

It is possible to represent the plates which make up the shells of prawns, stone fly creepers and a few other patterns in two other ways: one, the back material may be tied in, in separate shaped sections with a few turns of body material between each plate; or, two, it may even be folded back on itself and held by the ribbing (Figure 15.5).

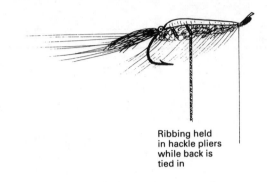

Ribbing held
in hackle pliers
while back is
tied in

Ribbing finished
over back as well
as body

Figure 15.4. Back of prawn fly.

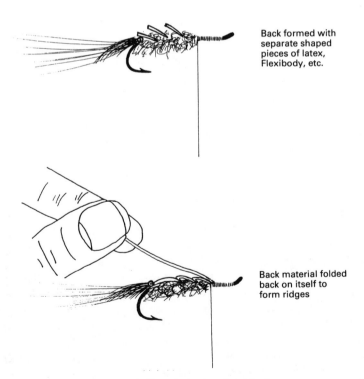

Back formed with
separate shaped
pieces of latex,
Flexibody, etc.

Back material folded
back on itself to
form ridges

Figure 15.5. Two alternative prawn backs.

An effective material for such backs is the marked sheets of wing material most commonly used on dry sedge patterns. The sheet is simply cut or burned to shape and tied in as above. The major advantage of this sheet is that it may be folded and the fold will remain.

Richard Walker's Mayfly Nymph, and only a very few other patterns, use Vycoat or varnish to simulate the back of the abdomen. I have never found applying varnish to wool or feather satisfactory. A thin strip of clear polythene will serve the same function with much neater results.

16 Legs

On most flies it is the hackle which suggests the presence of insect legs and their movement. Of course a wound hackle has many more fibres than the six or eight of the natural. For most flies accurate representation is unnecessary. The only exceptions possibly being when, for example, a natural's legs are unusually long, as with the Daddy Long Legs (Plate 10).

The traditional hackle offers an impressionistic image of legs, movement, a means of stabilising the fly in the water and, if required, the ability to float. In some cases, especially that of the parachute flies, it is not the hackle itself but the impression it makes in the surface film of water which gives the illusion of legs.

To construct the legs of a Daddy Long Legs cock pheasant centre tail fibres are most commonly used, but dyed nylon fishing line is much more durable. For each leg take a pair of cock pheasant fibres and tie a knot in each, sometimes two knots. Tying the knots takes time. It helps to make a loop in the fibres and pull one end through it with tweezers. Knots tied in this way will realistically show joints. I prefer double knots on my own Daddy Long Legs for durability. The legs may be tied in separately in the correct positions. Richard Walker's version is more practical for normal casting as the legs trail back under the body. Two knots are used as insurance against a break. Hawthorn fly legs and bee legs (Plate 10) are made in the same way except that black feather fibre, or nylon natural or dyed is used.

Exactly the same material, prepared as above, may be used for the 'paddles' of a Corixa, and it has many other uses. Knots are not strictly necessary here. Stone fly nymphs may have a simple hackle or more strikingly knotted goose biots. The same procedure is followed as for pheasant tail but the biots are thick, springy and shorter which don't make the knots any easier (Figure 16.1).

Pieces of nylon line, stiff fibres from a paint brush and several other materials can be used as legs. Their importance, in most flies for deception, is questionable.

An effective representation of a water spider's legs is created with three or four peacock sword fibres (normally used for Alexandra wings) tied across the top of the hook and split apart with figure of eight turns. The ends are then cut to the required length. Though not very durable this representation looks well.

Some American patterns, such as the Girdle Bug, use long pieces of white rubber projecting out in all directions. Doubtless this adds considerable mobility to the fly but they look grotesque, and I confess to no experience of their use for fishing.

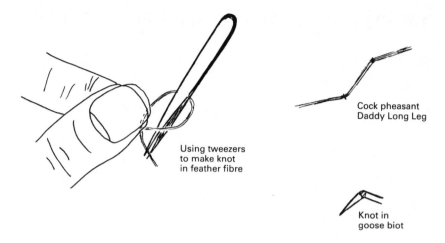

Using tweezers
to make knot
in feather fibre

Cock pheasant
Daddy Long Leg

Knot in
goose biot

Figure 16.1. Knotting legs.

Realism can be carried too far. I have seen some nymphs where six legs of bent nylon have been used. Many look realistic out of water but lack all mobility in the water. Such creations illustrate the difference between practical flytying for angling and tying for exhibition.

The 'wonder wing' technique is impractical but realistic looking and is used to construct some stone fly wings and even the legs of some grasshopper patterns. Draw some hackle feather fibres back towards the base of the stalk and then tie a knot around the stalk itself (see Figure 11.2). The remaining fibres at the tip of the hackle are stripped. The hackle stalk is then bent to form the knees and the whole leg is varnished. The process is time consuming and pointless in fishing terms, and a wing made in this way is hardly likely to last long (Figure 16.2).

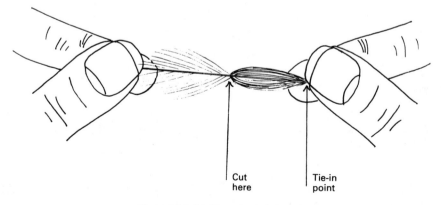

Cut
here

Tie-in
point

Figure 16.2. Making a 'wonder' wing.

17 Nymph Breathers

This is a rather loose term which covers the breathing tubes of midges and the gills of up-winged fly nymphs.

Modern representations of midge pupae (Plates 5 and 6) invariably include white tufts at either end to suggest breathing tubes, and there is a number of methods to achieve this.

The easiest method is to tie in white cock hackle fibres, or white floss silk, all along the top of the hook as the thread is wound down the shank and around the bend. When the fly is finished the material is clipped short at each end. In the case of the hackle fibres it is normal to have the tips of the hackle fibres at the bend and the thicker end at the hook eye. A turn or two of thread should ensure that the tuft at the eye points upwards, before the whip finish is made.

A variety of other materials, such as wool, antron, etc. may also be used especially if a larger tuft is required at the eye. As with Shipman's Buzzer and my SB patterns (Plates 2 and 3) these may be fluorescent. If so it is particularly important to make them small enough to be seen without dominating the rest of the fly.

The nymphs of the up-winged flies have gills along each side of the abdomen which are constantly in motion. These can be represented on large nymphs by tying a few strands of marabou along each side of the abdomen (Plate 9). Alternatively, if the abdomen is made of fur or wool, it may be picked out with a needle when the fly is complete, and this will serve the same function (Figure 17.1).

Whether or not a fish will be fooled by this attempt at imitation or is simply attracted by the extra movement and translucency of the fly is debatable and irrelevant — it works!

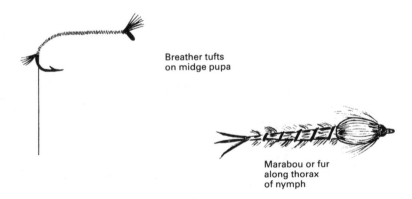

Breather tufts
on midge pupa

Marabou or fur
along thorax
of nymph

Figure 17.1. Breathers on papae and nymphs.

18 Veils

Veils are pieces of feather fibre tied closely over the body of some salmon flies. Traditionally toucan or indian crow are the most popular on the traditional dressings but it is impossible to obtain these now. I am not at all keen on the shop bought substitutes. There is, however, a simple and cheap solution which can look equally good.

Take a hen hackle of the correct shade (in the case of toucan, custard yellow). Make two or three turns of the hackle and a few more turns of thread over the bases of the fibres. This should make them lie close to the body. This hackle is separated on top and below the shank with figure of eight turns of thread though it may be bulky. Alternatively, a bunch of hackle fibres can be tied on the top and the bottom of the hook.

19 Feelers

Only a very few patterns call for feelers, notably some versions of realistic prawn. The standard procedure is to strip the fibres off four cock hackle stalks, dye them and tie them in at the bend of the hook. However lifelike these may appear, they do tend to be brittle and I much prefer a small bunch of bucktail.

20 Shucks

When a fly hatches through the surface film of water it leaves behind it the split skin of the nymph or pupa from which it emerged. This is the shuck.

As the insect is hatching it is very vulnerable to predators as it can neither swim or fly. For most insects this is a time of very rapid transition but some don't make it.

Simply using an extended tail of tippet or hair may help to suggest that the fly is in mid-hatch. Another, and rather more realistic, method is to tie in a few strands of nylon thread and melt the exposed end to prevent it from fraying. The fly may then be oiled with the shuck hanging beneath the surface film (Figure 20.1).

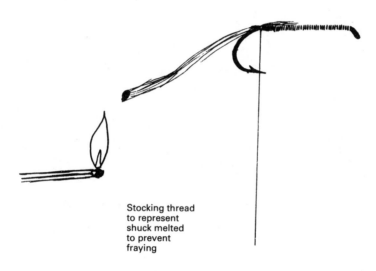

Stocking thread
to represent
shuck melted
to prevent
fraying

Figure 20.1. Representing a shuck.

21 Tandem Mount

The use of a tandem mount is a method of producing a long fly which is both light and flexible. It is most commonly used on sea trout and salmon flies (Plate 13). When constructing the mount (Figure 21.1) it should be remembered that the length may be adjusted by lengthening the gap between, rather than increasing the size of, the hooks. Also the rear hook may be dressed or left bare.

The best link between the hooks is nylon line of appropriate thickness, say, 10 to 15 lb depending on the hook size and the gap between them.

Hooks may also be threaded onto braided nylon to make tandems which are very neat and simple (Figure 21.1).

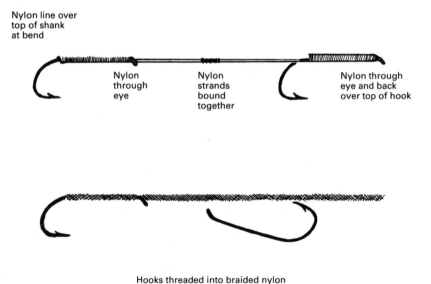

Figure 21.1. Constructing the tandem mount. Both types are secured with binding and glue.

22 Axis of the Hook

Depending on the way in which the fly is tied the hook may fish downwards, upwards or even horizontally. This is generally achieved by weighting the hook but not always. The following examples will illustrate the point.

Bead chain eyes may be tied on top or beneath the shank. If they are tied on top the hook will fish point upwards and vice versa. I prefer, where possible, to tie them on top because when tied underneath the gape of the hook can be partly shielded.

A realistic prawn fly tied on a double salmon hook (Plate 15) rarely fishes with hook points downwards, even when extra weight is added beneath the shank. This clearly is not because of the weight but because the hackles act as an underwater parachute and make it fish upside down. Its catching qualities do not seem to be harmed by this.

Some modern dead fry imitations are tied so that they lie on the water sideways thus enhancing the appearance of death. The fly is formed entirely of deer hair spun Muddler fashion but trimmed so that its shape is deep and narrow.

Thinking about how the fly will perform in, or on, the water is essential to the flytier who hopes to improve the catching qualities of his flies.

Part Two

QUALITIES OF FLIES

Durability

First let us consider what kind of punishment a fly may have to take. It is squashed and crumpled when being handled, air resistance damages the fly during casting, it is frequently dragged through overhanging trees, bushes and grass. All these take their toll and, in addition, there are occasions when the fly may even get wet and be chewed by a fish.

There are some people who would argue that such wear and tear is essential to increase the fly's effectiveness and they are probably right. You simply must decide where you stand on the durability question. You may feel, if you are able to do a lot of tying, that the extra time required to increase durability is not justified. I do a great deal of tying and fishing and have come to the conclusion that it is only worth the time for flies which are regularly in service.

Here are some tried and trusted ideas you might consider. I don't use them on every fly but with selective use they may be of value.

- There is no substitute for good strong even tying and good choice of material.
- Choose material of good quality.
- Make sure the thread is well waxed, without being over waxed. Use solid wax.
- The thread must be held tight at all times.
- Mostly a layer of thread must cover all parts of the hook where any material is to be tied in.
- Keep all materials taut when winding.
- Tie in as much scrap as possible.
- Wind everything evenly — especially ribbing.
- Where possible wind ribbing in opposite direction to body material.
- Wind thread through hackle fibres or cover base with thread.
- Develop a reasonable degree of skill.

All the above not only ensure strength but also can be used to enhance the profile of a fly. The scrap ends of dry fly wings for example, if cut correctly, will help to taper the body towards the tail.

All these and a few other hints have been mentioned already in Part One but there are additional methods of achieving durability. Purists of the more traditional methods may disapprove; however, the hints I give below do work.

No matter how careful we are there is always the risk of slipping or unravelling.

After each item is tied in a half hitch should prevent complete disintegration.

I first addressed the durability issue some years ago after a complaint from someone for whom I tied up a few Cinnamon and Golds. One fell to bits after having landed five good sea trout in one day. I saw no grounds for the complaint at all but it does illustrate that if a fly is to be used regularly it might be worth taking a little extra trouble, at least on flies for personal use.

Thin clear varnish or superglue are invaluable, particularly the latter. Both are excellent for cementing bodies of tinsel and herl but not for silk or wool, because the glue will soak through the material making it hard, rough and likely to change the colour. The latter, however, is no great problem as many wools and silk darken when wet but hardness and roughness are great drawbacks.

For tinsel or herl a small drop of glue is spread over the thread which is already covering the shank. The material is then wound over it in the normal way except that it will be impossible to unwind and start again if a mistake is made so care is needed. Once the body is ribbed a further drop or two of glue can be spread on top. I find this particularly useful on mylar tinsel bodies, which are easily damaged. The glue also ensures that the rib, if not quite perfect, will not slip.

The only real problem apart from the danger of glueing yourself to the body, is that you must wait for the glue to dry before continuing. I do several bodies at a time, finish each with a half hitch or whip finish and then leave them to dry. After several bodies are done the first should be ready for hackle and wings. Perhaps two applications of glue are a little more than necessary as the outer coat of glue is usually quite sufficient. Be careful not to use too much or it will drip into the eye of the hook (a devil of a job to get rid of), or will form discolouring bubbles between the turns of ribbing and tinsel. A strip of fine polythene wrapped over the body will do the same job but is less satisfactory.

Superglue is also very good for holding the roots of wings, especially those of coarse hair like bucktail or slippery hair like squirrel tail. Again very little glue is the key. Too much can clog the eye or soak through to the visible part of the wing or hackle making them rigid and lifeless.

Be careful at all times to ensure that durability does not become the prime factor in construction. Get the combination of material to do your job right and only then consider durability. If you think glue or its like will compromise the attractiveness of a fly, don't use it. Such situations are rare.

Materials and Colours

There are two things which you must always remember about flytying materials. First, in order to make perfectly good and successful flies there is no need to use the highest quality materials; second, almost anything can be used to make flies. Indeed, much of the fun of flytying is gained from being inventive (Plate 18).

These two points could be disputed by those who tie exhibition pieces, or those commercial tiers with a particular market to satisfy, but for the rest of us who tie flies for fun and as a means of catching fish they most certainly are true.

Much has been written about particular materials elsewhere in this book but the following points are worthy of attention.

More has been written about the quality of hackle feathers than any other material. By a 'high-quality cock hackle' we generally mean one with a long stalk and short fibres or flue. These fibres must be stiff and shiny. To obtain hackle capes of this type requires a lot of money. I own two such capes but I did not buy them, I won them in a flytying competition, and I don't expect to buy many more.

The reasons for this are quite simple: I could not afford a full stock of such capes; I tie and use relatively few dry flies for which much of the effort to obtain high-quality hackles has been directed; medium-quality hackles are invariably softer and so more mobile and lifelike; and modern floatants are so efficient that they largely remove the need for the 'best' hackles.

In short, the best quality hackles may not be the best for the purpose you require. Indeed there are many people, including myself, who would argue strongly that the softer and scruffier a fly is the more attractive it is likely to be. I use a lot of hen hackles and the soft feathers of partridge, grouse and woodcock for this reason.

Many of the bodies which I tie consist of two quite different types of material, reflective tinsel or lurex below and lightly dubbed and blended fur on top. The qualities of both combine to produce a very translucent body. Blending of the dubbing is particularly important, because blending a definite colour such as black or orange with a little hare or rabbit mellows the tone slightly. The resulting subdued more 'natural' look seems to me to be more in keeping with the trout's environment (Plate 2).

Seal's fur has traditionally been the basis of many fly dubbings but is now replaced with synthetics which are excellent substitutes. Some like Flyrite dubbing even have slight marbling of shade already mixed in. Synthetics certainly have a different texture. The fish do not seem to miss seal fur nearly as much as flytiers do.

If an unmellowed colour is needed you may find that embroidery wool will often suffice. It may be tied in a variety of thicknesses, is easy to use and is cheap.

I also make extensive use of fluorescent wools and flosses, but not often to wrap around the hook to form a body. I prefer to use these as tails or tags (Plates 2 and 3), they are more translucent and mobile that way. I doubt if it can be conclusively proved that fluorescence is a positive advantage but I am convinced that it is when used in small amounts.

It would be a mistake to over-stress the effectiveness of fluorescent materials. The fish, after all, do not see our flies in the same way as we do. Most flies are seen against the distorted background of sky, waves, etc.

The fish's colour vision has long been a subject for speculation and experiment. T. C. Kingsmill-Moore strongly believed that certain black materials were more attractive than others. In his book *A Man May Fish* (1983) he discussed the possible effectiveness of several black materials. He wrote about the special attraction which hare's ear, black ostrich and blue jay seemed to have for fish. I could not think of any fly which included all three materials and as a result the Trident (Plate 11) was born. I named it Trident because it used just the three materials and in its first season it proved to be as deadly as the missile, especially for brown and sea trout.

Marabou floss silk is excellent stuff. Unless you have a specific need for fluorescent floss you will require no other. Most synthetic flosses are not worthy of much attention. They tend to disintegrate, with long fibres tangling on the rest of the dressing as they are wound.

When wire is used it is invariably either gold or silver. I don't know why this should be so. I now have a stock of fine electrical wires of various colours: brown, green, red and various shades of copper. I use them extensively — the fish are certainly not put off by them — and I got them for free.

As I stated at the beginning almost anything can be used to make flies (Plate 18). I have used all sorts of material on flies which have all caught fish. With a little imagination you will doubtless find many more.

A few of my more successful flies have been constructed from oddities, or the scraps left on my bench after making more standard patterns. We should always try to be inventive or at least imaginative. In 1988 the Fly Dresser's Guild introduced an innovative category into its annual flytying competition. Out of a total membership of about 3,000 in the United Kingdom there were only five entries, none showing sufficient innovation in terms of materials or skills to be judged worthy of the trophy. This was a great pity. One glance at the photographs or flies in angling catalogues from the United States or the rest of Europe will suggest that we in the United Kingdom are either very conservative or just have very little imagination.

There are those people who argue that there is no need to innovate at all. On every water there seems to be someone who never bothers to change the flies on his cast throughout the season. Indeed, some of our most popular spider and palmered patterns were first developed several hundred years ago. There is no reason why these patterns should not continue to catch fish in the future, but nevertheless we do need to experiment.

Some eminent salmon anglers claim that the size of the fly is the only important factor in their choice of fly. Very few patterns are ever brand new creations; instead, old flies are reinvented, old techniques are adapted for new materials and only rarely does a fly combine new methods and materials. So why bother to innovate at all in terms of fly design?

The reasons why I try are very simple. First, I get immense satisfaction and fun out of experimenting and, second, like many other people, I am always searching for the fly which will catch more and catch when conditions are difficult. If a fly which never failed was created it would take all the fun out of fishing but since such a fly will never exist it is harmless fun to keep looking.

I have included plates of essential, useful, unnecessary and unorthodox materials. No one will agree totally with these selections but they suit me and if nothing else they ought to provoke a little thought. During the last twenty years I have collected a vast selection of material, much of which is only seen when it gets an annual dose of moth crystals to prevent it becoming infested. It is largely a waste of space and money.

Flytiers increasingly have a moral problem to face in terms of the material they use. We must recognise that fly fishing and flytying requires the death of a wide variety of other creatures before we begin. This may seem a rather blunt way of putting it but in the past this fact was either ignored altogether or accepted as making use of the by-products of the millinery and other trades. However, in the future much more thought will have to be given to the sources of the materials we use.

The general public is increasingly aware of the moral issues arising from the use of animal products. Everyone has mental images of baby seals being clubbed to death, elephant poaching in Africa and so on. As anglers who are primarily concerned with the survival of trout, salmon and their habitats, we must not be complacent about the sources of our flytying materials. Is it not hypocritical to complain about poaching of trout or salmon while using feathers from endangered species on the flies we use to catch them?

As responsible anglers and flytiers we really ought to anticipate the problems which may arise from such issues. Guidelines for flytiers on the sources of materials would be a useful beginning to keeping our house in order. The anti-angling lobby should not be given more ammunition than they think they already have, but it would be impossible for individual tiers to keep abreast of all the regulations on the subject.

Every flytier is aware that there is a ban on the import of jungle cock into the United Kingdom and that the only legal way of obtaining it is from birds which are bred in this country. There are, however, a great many more items which are covered by import regulations, parliamentary wildlife and countryside acts, directives from the European Commission (EC) and so on. The situation is further complicated by goods which can be traded between EC countries and goods imported to EC countries, not to mention the varying strictness with which restrictions are enforced.

We should be made aware of, and be sensitive to, the consequences of our demands as flytiers and, where necessary, be prepared to use more environmentally friendly materials. After all, there is no shortage of them.

Dyeing

I find it increasingly unnecessary to dye flytying materials. The range of materials on offer from dealers (some of whom will dye to order if you provide a sample of what you require) is so wide these days.

Dyeing is a tedious and messy business anyway. Feathers must be washed, degreased, dyed and dried which is a waste of time and space. The amateur may find it difficult to obtain the correct shade anyway. I once tried to dye deer hair black and achieved a dull green olive instead!

I find only two forms of dyeing which are useful: in one, prawn flies ought to be the same shade throughout but it is sometimes difficult to find fur, hackles, etc. all with exactly the same shade so the answer is to dye the fly after it has been tied; in the other, felt-tip pens are useful if only a part of a feather is to be coloured, but even these are rarely used.

Proportions

We can never view flies wholly from the fish's perspective but that should not prevent us from trying to get close.

First hold the fly above your head and look at it as a fish usually will have to, against a bright sky or a cloudy sky. In both cases the translucency or solidity of the fly becomes obvious, also the range of colours which can be seen clearly diminish against the brighter background.

Then look at the fly with moving traffic as the background. Water will tend, even when still, to distort and move this background to a greater or lesser extent depending on the conditions.

A human being looking at an object against a background sees the object in relation to the background and not separate from it. It is reasonable to assume that a fish's eye works similarly in this respect. A fish's view is, however, distorted by refraction. The water may be coloured by peat or algae which must alter distance vision as well as adding a new element to the background. Depending on the depth and colour of the water most of the surface may appear to mirror the bottom of the river or loch so it is even possible for a fish to see the artificial fly and its reflection simultaneously. Water will also tend to support each fibre of the fly and its mobility will look rather different in still or running water rather than air.

Fish are well able to cope with all the permutations in their environment — if they could not they would not survive. My point is that as flytiers and anglers we should not judge a pattern as it appears to us. Given all the things which will interfere with the fish's view of our creations, how often do minute alterations to patterns really influence the success of an artificial fly? Rarely I think.

Exaggeration is a well-tried technique which is present in all representations of natural creatures to some extent; for example, the eyes of some fry patterns, wings on the G & H Sedge and the fan wings of Mayflies, but it would be impossible to prove that this single feature was the trigger for a take.

Usually I think it is best for us to build in proportions which suit the water or our style of fishing and let the fish worry about the rest.

There are simply too many aspects of proportions to mention them all. What follows below is a few examples which are worthy of attention on both practical and aesthetic terms.

One of the problems which is often more critical to the salmon and sea trout angler than the trout angler is keeping the fly on an even keel. This can be achieved in several ways. Basically, the larger the fly the more difficult it is to keep the fly level. Fishing downstream in fast water or by retrieving quickly helps, but these options are not always possible. The slower the water the smaller and bushier are the flies I use. With Waddington and tube flies, even in fast water, it is always advisable to use small trebles which will not tip the fly backwards.

A question which may be common to both salmon and trout anglers is where the hook should be in relation to the dressing. In the case of sea trout flies it is usually advisable to tie the fly 'within the hook' meaning that no part of the dressing is allowed to extend beyond the bend of the hook. This is useful due to the fish's tendency to nip at a fly without being hooked. Tying the fly with a 'flying' hook can help but is in no way foolproof. The salmon angler has traditionally overcome the same problem by employing the low-water style but in both cases the modern tendency is to use small slimly dressed doubles and trebles.

The opposite extreme is illustrated by the Collie Dog where the hair extends at least twice the length of the hook or tube. Even for standard hair wing salmon flies there are those dressers who advocate wings twice the normal length. The added mobility which the longer hair offers may indeed help to attract fish but why should the fish not tug at the tail end of the dressing without getting hooked? Perhaps this is due to the fish turning on certain lengths of bait to take them head first.

Trout flies with extended dressings can also prove to be excellent hookers. Some patterns like the Sweeny Todd use a flash of fluorescent wool or floss near the eye of the hook as if it were an aiming point for the fish. This could not be said of a Ke-He, a pattern which I have consistently found to hook deep despite the bright 'target' being at the bend of the hook. One explanation for this is that the tail of the artificial suggests not the natural's tail but the shuck of a hatching insect. Presumably the trout learns that the meat is beyond the 'tail' and aims accordingly.

My 'Swedish Mayfly' uses the long fibred hackle from a French partridge but this has little to do with attempting to recreate the natural. Instead the long hackle, combined with the fan wings and long tail enable this fly to parachute to the water so that it always lands upright. Once on the water the fibres sit on the surface film dimpling it like the natural but over a much wider area. This keeps the hook point above the water surface and helps to hide it. Unfortunately the fish needs to rise a little higher to get hooked.

The fishing qualities of many dry flies may suffer from having long hackles which tend to make them roll around on the surface, but it is difficult to see how many wet flies could suffer from having hackles which are out of proportion.

It is very easy for the inexperienced flytier to become preoccupied with trying to recreate the proportions of tails, hackle and wing of traditional patterns. This wastes much time and effort. If the fly holds together long enough to catch fish what else is needed?

The average beginner would be better advised to avoid overdoing the overall bulk of the fly. This is certainly true of adding weight to the fly. Even some professionals overdo weight which only leads to difficult and dangerous casting.

It is a very worthwhile exercise to tie one fly pattern with a selection of tail, hackle, wing and body proportions, then tie them to nylon line and look at them in water. You will then have some justification for preferring a particular style but much more importantly it will give you a hint as to the behaviour of the fly when it is twenty yards or more away from you in a river or loch.

My Choice of Flies

Over the last twenty years I have tied just about every type of fly which I have seen. During this period I have had experience of a wide range of angling situations but the vast majority of my time has been spent in the following ways:

BROWN TROUT   From 15 March until June my fishing is almost exclusively for loch brown trout. The lochs vary greatly in size, altitude and acidity but the trout are almost all natural, wild and modest in size

SEA TROUT   From June or July, depending on the rain which is vital for the lightning fast spate rivers which I mostly fish, sea trout begin to run and can be taken on fly as the spate clears or after dark in low water

SALMON   From July until the end of October every rise and fall of water may offer the chance of salmon. During this time salmon takes precedence over everything else, except when the river conditions are poor when I revert to fishing for brown trout.

My ideas about flies have been developed primarily for these three situations so I have confined my writing on fly types and construction to them. My experience does extend over a greater range but not on a regular enough basis for me to claim any deep insight.

I have studied the flies used for all three situations for a number of years with a view to producing a definitive set of flies for each which would be capable of catering for every possibility. This has been a very difficult task to which I have returned at regular intervals, beginning every new season with a fresh batch of ideas and flies. I have passed the stage of carrying every fly I could think of lest I have the excuse for failure of not having the correct pattern. At one time I regularly took seven full fly boxes on every trip to the water.

I lingered for a shorter period with the notion that only half-a-dozen patterns were enough to cover every eventuality. I know a number of anglers who are quite happy with this limited range of flies but I was never comfortable with it. Perhaps this can be partly accounted for by the fact that I had amassed such a huge collection of flytying materials by this stage that I had to justify the expense somehow.

These two extremes are now firmly in the past. My approach is much more logical and practical now and, although I am always experimenting, I do not expect to make radical changes in the future.

The long process of developing these sets of flies for stillwater brown trout, sea trout and salmon began by assessing the qualities of my most successful patterns and trying to deduce why these qualities were important. The results for all three were as follows:

Visibility

Obviously a fly which is not seen will not be taken but I firmly believe that some artificials are much too visible. Gaudy flies may be highly effective when we wish to inflame the aggression of a fish but this is only one motivation for a take. I prefer flies which do not look too out of place. Visibility can be achieved simply by increasing the size of the fly by including bright materials but any attempt to increase visibility must take account of water and weather conditions. For example, I have always found blue flies such as the Donegal Blue (Plate 11), to be particularly effective for trout on misty days.

Mobility

It is mobility which gives an artificial the impression of life and even if we are not trying to represent a specific creature it is movement which distinguishes the artificial from all the inert debris which drifts past the fish.

Translucency

To a greater or lesser degree this quality is present in every creature preyed upon by trout in freshwater or by salmon and sea trout in the sea. It is quite impossible to recreate this on a solid hook but it is possible to suggest it in several ways.

Generally representative

The more exact your representations of natural creatures the more patterns you will need and the greater your knowledge of entomology must be. Neither of these are needed. Even without small adjustments to a dressing a single fly may be able to represent a wide range of naturals. For example, the Gold Ribbed Hare's Ear (Plate 8) is capable of representing a wide variety of up-wing nymphs and even sedges, simply by varying its size. The suggestion of life is created without being too specific.

With some sea trout and salmon flies the position is often different in that we hope to suggest a particular creature — fish, shrimp, or prawn — by offering it the merest outline. Examples of this would be the Medicine (Plate 13) and traditional shrimp flies (Plate 15). Any fly which is indefinite in colour and profile is worth a try.

Versatile

The vast majority of my trout fishing is with wet flies. However, there are occasions especially during Caenis, midge and sedge hatches when I may fish dry. It would be convienient then, if some of my wet flies could double as dry flies.

Shaggy

Most flies end up in this condition and it is often claimed that the oldest, scruffiest flies work best. So, why not use patterns which have this quality built in already?

Aesthetic

If I am not happy with the look of a fly I find it difficult to fish it with confidence, even though I know that what I like is of no interest to the fish.

Durability

This is an essential requirement of all flies, up to a point. Look at any fly which has been designed solely for durability and it will invariably look hard and lifeless. A fly which stays intact long enough to land a couple of fish owes you nothing. Being soft and attractive has a much higher priority.

Range

There must be a sufficient range of patterns to cover all the angling situations which I am likely to meet in a season, without the need to carry seven fly boxes. The ideal is one box for each type of fishing.

Simplicity

I like the flies which I use regularly to be relatively simple and quick to tie so that they may be replaced easily and if they are made from cheap commonly available materials so much the better.

The above ideas have formed the basis of my thinking on flies for loch trout, sea trout and salmon. My own SBs (Plate 2) were first developed to cater for loch trout. These initials stand for Shaggy because this is one of their most important qualities; as for the B, the ideas which went into these flies came from such a wide variety of sources that they are of doubtful parentage. If you are too young or polite for such words — Beasts will do!

I have been converted to using grub hooks for the majority of my loch flies. No natural insect has a perfectly rigid body so if there is a way to avoid this on an artificial, why not?

Visibility is enhanced by using fluorescent floss tails in the style of Shipman's Buzzer. Provided that these are fine and small they will not overpower the fly. I have experimented with single tails at either end and found that there was little difference in their ability to attract fish. However, I am convinced that flies with both tails are better hookers.

Every part of the dressing is very mobile and combines in the water in a very lifelike fashion. The long-fibred dubbing for the bodies and soft hackles are common to all but deer hair, Palmer hackles and marabou tails. These latter three, with their varying degrees of softness, add to the effect. The soft hackle is a replacement for the typical wet fly wing which is the first part of the fly to disintegrate.

The natural translucency of fur bodies is increased by using an underbody of tinsel or lurex which shines through the body helping it to glow. SBs have a vaguely insect-like appearance. It is possible to associate success with one pattern to a particular hatch of fly. But 'matching the hatch' is a much less critical technique when using flies with as much in-built life as these.

An important part of the illusion is the blending of the fur. Few naturals on the trout's menu match the single vivid colours of many artificials. Blending the chosen colour with hare fur mellows it and is a little more realistic. I usually dub the fur on a thread which is the colour of the dubbing.

In small sizes the standard SB will sink or float as required; on the larger sizes deer hair is needed, but these are also fished wet to simulate emerging midges, duns and sedges. Weight below the body will increase the sink rate at the expense of a bulky body. When weighted at the eye of the hook it is fished Dog Nobbler style — sink and draw.

All SBs look very shaggy and have the minimum of outline. Armed with these flies you don't have to wait for them to become tatty. Not only do these flies look good, especially when they are looked at against the light, but they are extremely durable when a little varnish is applied to the underbody before winding the dubbing.

Choice of fly is relatively simple. I simply use an SB which is reasonably close in colour to any insect which I can see or should expect to see. I may use one with a blueish tint on overcast days or a reddish pattern in coloured water. If I can think of no reason to choose a particular colour I simply revert to a stand-by cast of black on the point, claret in the middle and yellow on the bob fly. The standard size is 12, which is increased as the water becomes rougher and is decreased in calm conditions.

Having a reason for using a fly and following a few simple rules for its use is my key to success on hill lochs.

Many of the same basic ideas govern the construction of my sea trout flies (Plate 3). Here I prefer a hook with a straight shank because I wish the fly to 'swim' on an even keel when fished, across and downstream in traditional style. Tinsel is an important ingredient for most sea trout flies, so about half of the underbody is left exposed in the style of a Peter Ross (Plate 11). The sparse cock hackle helps to give the fly stability in the water and the bronze mallard is as close to a hair wing as you can get with a feather.

Any standard pattern may be converted to this style. They may be tied on doubles, tandems and salmon fly hooks. I regularly use these as droppers when salmon fishing.

My salmon fly box holds two quite different styles of fly (Plates 13, 14 and 15). First, there are the simplified patterns which may retain the names of traditional built wing flies but are now nothing more than a bare hook or tube with a simple blend of bucktail, or squirrel or hackle fibre. There is nothing simpler or more effective. In one evening it is possible to produce a range of salmon flies of different colours and on different hooks and mounts to cater for your needs from spring to autumn.

However effective such flies are, I am much more interested in the second type which my box holds as these represent the shrimps and prawns on which the salmon once fed at sea. All the patterns (Plate 15) fall into this category, but why should there be such a range of shapes and colours? I suspect that it is the shape of the realistic pattern which produces a response, whereas the mobility of the traditional is its trigger.

Both these types of fly are fished on an intermediate or slow sinking line in summer and autumn. However, the traditional is at its best when it is worked in the water to make the dressing pulsate. The realistic version is allowed to swing round in the current like any other salmon fly. Interestingly, both usually produce the same heavy take.

Both types of shrimp may be tied in a range of colours. Red, orange and purple are the most common for the realistic versions but the traditional pattern has many more permutations. At the last count I have collected or produced ninety different patterns, though I have only three favourites (Plate 15).

Armed with these selections of brown trout, sea trout and salmon flies, with room in each box for peacock flies and a few 'jokers' you will have everything you need to catch fish regularly.

Appendix

FLY PATTERNS

AS ILLUSTRATED ON PLATES

Front Cover

NAMELESS

HOOK	– Partridge Bartleet code CS10 size 6
THREAD	– Black
TAG	– Gold oval and fluorescent orange floss
TAIL	– Lady Amherst pheasant red crest
BUTT	– Black ostrich
BODY REAR 2/5	– Gold tinsel
BODY FRONT 3/5	– Mixed seal sub: purple, pale green and yellow
FRONT BODY HACKLE	– Red cock
THROAT HACKLE	– Guinea fowl dyed red and blue
WING	– Lady Amherst pheasant tail
	– Married goose shoulder: yellow, orange and red
	– Bronze mallard
SIDES	– Jungle cock
CHEEKS	– Kingfisher
HEAD	– Black

Plate 2
SBs FOR LOCH TROUT

HOOKS — Partridge Grub code K4A size 18–2

STANDARD PATTERN – VIVA

THREAD	– Black
TAILS	– Fluorescent lime floss
UNDERBODY	– Green lurex
BODY	– Black seal sub mixed with hare
RIB	– Gold or silver wire
HACKLE	– Waterhen wing covert

PALMER PATTERN – GROUSE AND CLARET

THREAD	– Red
TAILS	– Fluorescent red floss
UNDERBODY	– Red lurex
BODY	– Claret seal sub mixed with hare
RIB	– Gold, silver or copper wire
BODY HACKLE	– Claret cock
HACKLE	– Grouse wing covert

EMERGER/DRY PATTERN – WOODCOCK AND YELLOW

THREAD	– Yellow
TAILS	– Fluorescent yellow floss
UNDERBODY	– Gold lurex
BODY	– Yellow seal sub mixed with hare
RIB	– Gold wire
HACKLE	– Woodcock wing covert
WING	– Deer hair

GOLDHEAD/LURE PATTERN – GROUSE AND ORANGE

HEAD	– Brass bead
THREAD	– Red
TAIL	– Fluorescent orange floss
	– Hot orange marabou
	– Lureflash twinkle
UNDERBODY	– Gold lurex
BODY	– Hot orange seal sub mixed with hare
RIB	– Gold or copper wire
HACKLE	– Grouse wing covert

Plate 3
SBs FOR SEA TROUT AND SALMON

HOOKS — Partridge Captain Hamilton code L2A size 12–4

BLACK AND SILVER

THREAD	– Black
TAIL	– Fluorescent yellow wool
REAR BODY	– Silver tinsel
FRONT UNDERBODY	– Silver tinsel
FRONT BODY	– Black seal sub mixed with hare
RIB	– Silver oval
THROAT	– Fluorescent yellow wool
HACKLE	– Black cock
WING	– Bronze mallard

GOLDEN OLIVE

THREAD	– Yellow
TAIL	– Fluorescent yellow wool
REAR BODY	– Gold tinsel
FRONT UNDERBODY	– Gold tinsel
FRONT BODY	– Golden olive seal sub mixed with hare
RIB	– Gold oval
THROAT	– Fluorescent yellow wool
HACKLE	– Golden olive cock
WING	– Bronze mallard

COPPER AND ORANGE

THREAD	– Red
TAIL	– Fluorescent orange wool
REAR BODY	– Copper tinsel
FRONT UNDERBODY	– Copper tinsel
FRONT BODY	– Hot orange seal sub mixed with hare
RIB	– Twisted copper wire
THROAT	– Fluorescent orange wool
HACKLE	– Cinnamon cock
WING	– Bronze mallard

MAGENTA AND RED

THREAD	– Red
TAIL	– Fluorescent magenta wool
REAR BODY	– Red lurex
FRONT UNDERBODY	– Red lurex
FRONT BODY	– Claret seal sub mixed with hare
RIB	– Twisted red copper wire
THROAT	– Fluorescent magenta wool
HACKLE	– Magenta cock
WING	– Bronze mallard

Plate 4
PEACOCK FLIES

BLACK AND PEACOCK SPIDER

HOOK	– Partridge Captain Hamilton code L2A size 16–8
THREAD	– Black
BODY	– Bronze peacock herls twisted with silver wire
HACKLE	– Black cock or hen

PEACOCK STICK FLY

HOOK	– Partridge Captain Hamilton code L2A size 14–8
THREAD	– Black
BODY	– Bronze peacock herls twisted with silver wire
ABDOMEN	– Fluorescent white wool
HACKLE	– Black cock or hen

BLACK KE-HE

HOOK	– Partridge Captain Hamilton code L2A size 16–6
THREAD	– Black
TAIL	– Golden pheasant tippet and fluorescent lime wool
BODY	– Bronze peacock herls twisted with silver wire
HACKLE	– Black cock

WORM FLY

HOOK	– Partridge Bucktail/Streamer code D4A size 14–6
REAR BODY	– Bronze peacock herls twisted with copper wire
TAIL	– Fluorescent lime wool
MIDDLE HACKLE	– Black cock or hen
FRONT BODY	– Bronze peacock herls twisted with copper wire
FRONT HACKLE	– Black cock or hen

GOAT'S TOE

HOOK	– Partridge Albert code A size 10–8
THREAD	– Black
TAIL	– Red wool
BODY	– Bronze peacock herls twisted with wire
HACKLE	– Peacock blue neck

Plate 5
LIFELESS FLIES

MIDGE PUPA

HOOK	– Partridge Sproat code G3A size 16–10
THREAD	– Black
BREATHERS	– White floss
ABDOMEN	– Red and black feather fibre — mixed
RIB	– White thread
BREATHERS	– White antron
THORAX	– Bronze peacock herl

CORIXA

HOOK	– Partridge Sproat code G3A size 12–8
THREAD	– Yellow
UNDERBODY	– Lead wire
TAG	– Silver tinsel
BODY	– White floss
RIB	– Silver tinsel
BACK	– Brown feather fibre varnished
BEARD	– Brown cock fibres
'LEGS'	– Cock pheasant centre tail
HEAD	– Yellow thread

PHEASANT TAIL NYMPH

HOOK	– Partridge Sproat code G3A size 16–12
'THREAD'	– Copper wire
UNDER THORAX	– Copper wire
TAIL	– Cock pheasant centre tail
ABDOMEN	– Cock pheasant centre tail

PHEASANT TAIL NYMPH *continued*
WING CASES   – Cock pheasant centre tail
THORAX   – Cock pheasant centre tail
HEAD   – Copper wire

STICK FLY
HOOK   – Partridge Bucktail/Streamer code D4A size 14–8
THREAD   – Black
BODY   – Cock pheasant centre tail mixed with olive feather fibre
ABDOMEN   – Amber antron
HACKLE   – Ginger hen

Plate 6
MIDGES

BLOODWORM
HOOK   – Partridge Grub Hook code K4A size 12–8
THREAD   – Red
WEIGHT   – Near eye
TAIL   – Red marabou
UNDERBODY   – Gold lurex
BODY   – Red seal sub
RIB   – Gold wire

HATCHING PUPA
HOOK   – Partridge Albert code A size 16–10
THREAD   – Black
BREATHERS   – Fluorescent white floss
ABDOMEN   – Orange feather fibre
RIB   – Silver wire
THORAX   – Mole

DUCK FLY
HOOK   – Partridge Grub Hook code K4A size 14–10
THREAD   – Black
BODY   – Olive wool
RIB   – Silver wire
WINGS   – Starling
HACKLE   – Olive cock

ADULT MIDGE
HOOK   – Partridge Captain Hamilton code L3B size 18–14
THREAD   – Black
ABDOMEN   – Black floss
WING   – Medium blue dun cock hackle fibres
THORAX   – Mole
WING CASES   – Dark feather fibre
HACKLE   – Black cock

Plate 7
SEDGE/CADDIS FLIES

LARVA
HOOK   – Partridge Bucktail/Streamer code D4A size 12–8
THREAD   – Black
WEIGHT   – Along shank
BODY CASE   – Hare
RIB   – Gold oval

LARVA *continued*
ABDOMEN	– Fluorescent yellow wool
HACKLE	– Waterhen wing covert

PUPA
HOOK	– Partridge Bucktail/Streamer code D4A size 14–12
THREAD	– Black
ABDOMEN	– Orange seal sub
RIB	– Silver tinsel
THORAX	– Dark brown feather fibre
WING CASES	– Mottled feather fibre
HACKLE	– Fluorescent cream hen

HATCHING PUPA-LONGHORN
HOOK	– Partridge Albert code A size 14–10
THREAD	– Yellow
BODY	– Olive antron
RIB	– Gold oval
THORAX	– Cinnamon ostrich herl
ANTENNAE	– Cock pheasant tail
HACKLE	– Brown partridge

ADULT SEDGE
HOOK	– Partridge Captain Hamilton code L3B size 14–8
THREAD	– Black
BODY	– Cream seal sub mixed with hare
RIB	– Lureflash mobile
WINGS	– Rolled cock pheasant wing fibre
HACKLE	– Natural red cock

Plate 8
UP-WING FLIES

NYMPH
HOOK	– Partridge Captain Hamilton code L2A size 16–12
THREAD	– Black
TAIL	– Dark olive cock
BODY	– Grey feather fibre dyed olive
THORAX	– Mixed seal sub brown and golden olive
WING CASES	– Cinnamon feather fibre
HACKLE	– Fluorescent fawn hen

HATCHING HARE'S EAR VARIANT
HOOK	– Partridge Captain Hamilton code L2A size 16–12
THREAD	– Yellow
BODY	– Hare
RIB	– Gold wire
WING	– Elk hair

PHEASANT BLUE DUN
HOOK	– Partridge Captain Hamilton code L3B size 16–12
THREAD	– Black
TAIL	– Medium blue dun cock
BODY	– Cock pheasant tail
WINGS	– Starling
HACKLE	– Medium blue dun cock

CAENIS SPINNER
HOOK	– Partridge Captain Hamilton code L3B size 18–14
THREAD	– Black

CAENIS SPINNER   *continued*
TAIL   – Nylon paint brush fibres
BODY   – Cream angora wool
WINGS   – Pearl Lureflash
THORAX   – Mole
OPTIONAL HACKLE   – Badger cock

Plate 9
REPRESENTATIVE WET FLIES

MAYFLY NYMPH
HOOK   – Partridge Bucktail/Streamer code D4A size 10–6
THREAD   – Black
WEIGHT   – Along hook
TAIL   – Cock pheasant tail
ABDOMEN   – Cream angora wool
BREATHERS   – Amber marabou
RIB   – Copper wire
THORAX   – Cream angora wool
WING CASES   – Cock pheasant tail
LEGS   – Cock pheasant tail

DAMSEL FLY NYMPH
HOOK   – Partridge Bucktail/Streamer code D4A size 10–6
WEIGHT   – Along shank
TAIL   – Olive marabou
ABDOMEN   – Olive seal sub
RIB   – Gold oval
THORAX   – Mixed brown and olive seal sub
HACKLE   – Brown partridge dyed olive
WING CASES   – Brown feather fibre

FRESHWATER SHRIMP
HOOK   – Partridge Grub code K4A size 12–8
THREAD   – Black
WEIGHT   – On top of shank
'TAILS'   – Fox squirrel
BODY   – Mixed olive, golden olive and orange seal sub
BACK   – Brown flexibody
RIB   – Gold wire

PEARLSTICKLE
HOOK   – Partridge Bucktail/Streamer code D4A size 10–6
THREAD   – Black
WEIGHT   – Along shank
BODY   – Pearl Lureflash
BACK AND TAIL   – Black Lureflash

Plate 10
REPRESENTATIVE DRY FLIES

DADDY LONG LEGS
HOOK   – Partridge Nymph Hook code H1A size 12
THREAD   – Black
BODY   – Rolled rubber glue
LEGS   – Six pairs of cock pheasant tail fibres knotted twice
WINGS   – Cree cock hackles
HACKLE   – Natural red cock

MAYFLY – SWEDISH
HOOK — Partridge Swedish Dry Fly code K3A size 16–12
THREAD — Black
TAIL — Cock pheasant tail
BODY — Buff feather fibre with two bands of cock pheasant near the tail
WINGS — Male mallard breast dyed yellow
HACKLES — French partridge dyed golden olive on top of golden olive cock
HEAD — Peacock herl

COW DUNG
HOOK — Partridge Captain Hamilton Dry Fly code L3B size 14–10
THREAD — Black
BODY — Mixed golden olive and olive seal sub
RIB — Gold oval or wire
WINGS — Polythene scraped with sandpaper and dyed with dark grey felt-tip pen
HACKLE — Natural red cock

BLACK GNAT
HOOK — Partridge Albert Dry code B size 16–14
THREAD — Black
BODY — Black floss
WINGS — Polythene
HACKLE — Black cock

HAWTHORN FLY
HOOK — Partridge Albert Dry code B size 14–12
THREAD — Black
BODY — Black floss
LEGS — Knotted nylon dyed black
OPTIONAL WINGS — Medium blue dun cock hackle fibres
HACKLE — Black cock

Plate 11
GENERAL WET FLIES

INVICTA
HOOK — Partridge McHaffie Master code MM1B size 10–4
THREAD — Black
TAIL — Golden pheasant crest and ibis sub
BODY — Yellow antron yarn
RIB — Gold oval or wire
BODY HACKLE — Natural red cock
THROAT — Blue jay
WING — Hen pheasant tail

SOLDIER PALMER
HOOK — Partridge McHaffie Master code MM1B size 10–8
THREAD — Black
OPTIONAL TAIL — Red wool
BODY — Red wool or dubbing
RIB — Gold oval or wire
BODY HACKLE — Natual red cock

CONNEMARA BLACK

HOOK	– Partridge McHaffie Master code MM1B size 10–4
THREAD	– Black
TAIL	– Golden pheasant crest
BODY	– Black seal sub
RIB	– Silver oval or wire
BODY HACKLE	– Black cock
THROAT	– Blue jay
WING	– Bronze mallard

SOOTY OLIVE

HOOK	– Partridge McHaffie Master code MM1B size 10–4
THREAD	– Black
TAIL	– Golden pheasant tippet
BODY	– Dark olive green seal sub
RIB	– Gold oval or wire
HACKLE	– Dark olive
WING	– Bronze mallard

DONEGAL BLUE

HOOK	– Partridge Albert code A size 14–8
THREAD	– Black
BODY	– Pale blue seal sub
RIB	– Silver oval or wire
HACKLE	– Black cock or hen

MUDDLER MINNOW VARIANT

HOOK	– Partridge Bucktail/Streamer code D4A size 10–6
THREAD	– Black
TAIL	– Golden pheasant crest
BODY	– Gold tinsel
RIB	– Gold oval
WING	– Orange and purple squirrel tail
HEAD	– Deer hair

PEARL INVICTA

HOOK	– Partridge Captain Hamilton code L2A size 14–6
THREAD	– Black
TAIL	– Fluorescent wool
BODY	– Pearl Lureflash
RIB	– Silver oval or wire
BODY HACKLE	– Natural red cock
THROAT	– Blue jay
WING	– Hen pheasant tail

MINI-MUDDLER

HOOK	– Partridge Captain Hamilton code L2A size 14–8
THREAD	– Black
TAIL	– Fluorescent lime wool
BODY	– Olive seal sub
RIB	– Gold wire
OPTIONAL BODY HACKLE	– Green olive cock
HEAD	– Deer hair

WICKHAM'S FANCY

HOOK	– Partridge sproat code G3A size 14–6
THREAD	– Black
TAIL	– Natural red cock fibres
BODY	– Gold lurex
RIB	– Gold oval or wire

WICKHAM'S FANCY   *continued*
BODY HACKLE   – Natural red cock
WING   – Grey mallard wing

HARE'S EAR VARIANT
HOOK   – Partridge McHaffie Master code MM1B size 16–4
THREAD   – Black
TAIL   – Dark natural red cock fibres
BODY   – Hare's ear
RIB   – Gold oval or wire
HACKLE   – Dark natural red cock
WING   – Grey mallard wing

BUTCHER
HOOK   – Partridge McHaffie Master code MM1B size 10–4
THREAD   – Black
TAIL   – Ibis sub
BODY   – Silver tinsel
RIB   – Silver oval or wire
HACKLE   – Black cock
WING   – Blue mallard wing

CLARET BUMBLE
HOOK   – Partridge Sproat code G3A size 14–8
THREAD   – Red
TAIL   – Golden pheasant tippet
BODY   – Claret seal sub
RIB   – Gold oval or wire
BODY HACKLES   – Claret and black cock
COLLAR   – Blue jay

PETER ROSS
HOOK   – Partridge Albert code A size 14–8
THREAD   – Black
TAIL   – Golden pheasant tippet
REAR BODY   – Silver tinsel
FRONT BODY   – Red seal sub
RIB   – Silver oval or wire
HACKLE   – Black cock
WING   – Teal

TRIDENT AND TRIDENT WITH FLYING HOOK
HOOK   – Partridge Captain Hamilton code L2A size 14–6
THREAD   – Yellow
REAR BODY   – Hare
RIB   – Gold oval or wire
FRONT BODY   – Black ostrich
HACKLE   – Blue jay

Plate 12
LURES

WHISKY FLY
HOOK   – Partridge Bucktail/Streamer code D4A size 10–4
THREAD   – Black
BODY   – Gold tinsel
RIB   – Fluorescent hot orange wool
HACKLE   – Hot orange cock
WING   – Hot orange bucktail

JACK FROST

HOOK	– Partridge Bucktail/Streamer code D4A size 10–4
THREAD	– Black
TAIL	– Fluorescent red wool
BODY	– Fluorescent white wool
WING	– White marabou
HACKLES	– White and red cock

BLACK CAT'S WHISKER

HOOK	– Partridge Bucktail/Streamer code D4A size 10–4
THREAD	– Black
EYES	– Bead chain
TAIL	– Black marabou
BODY	– Fluorescent lime chenille
RIB	– Gold oval
WING	– Black marabou

JERSEY HERD

HOOK	– Partridge Bucktail/Streamer code D4A size 10–4
THREAD	– Black
WEIGHT	– Along shank
BODY	– Copper tinsel
BACK AND TAIL	– Peacock herls
HEAD	– Peacock herl

MONTANA NYMPH

HOOK	– Partridge Bucktail/Streamer code D4A size 10–4
WEIGHT	– Along shank or under thorax
TAIL	– Black cock hackle fibres
ABDOMEN	– Black chenille
THORAX	– Fluorescent lime or yellow chenille
THORAX HACKLE	– Black cock
WING CASES	– Black chenille

Plate 13
LARGE SALMON AND SEA TROUT FLIES

THUNDER AND LIGHTNING

HOOK	– Partridge Salmon Single code M size 9/0
THREAD	– Black
TAG	– Gold oval and lemon floss
TAIL	– Golden pheasant crest and ibis sub
BUTT	– Black ostrich
BODY	– Black wool
RIB	– Gold oval
BODY HACKLE	– Orange cock
COLLAR HACKLE	– Blue guinea fowl
WING	– Brown bucktail
CHEEKS	– Jungle cock
TOPPING	– Golden pheasant crest
HEAD	– Black

BLUE CHARM

HOOK	– Partridge Low-Water code N size 9/0
THREAD	– Black
TAG	– Silver tinsel and yellow floss
TAIL	– Golden pheasant crest
BODY	– Black wool
RIB	– Silver oval

BLUE CHARM *continued*

THROAT HACKLE	– Blue cock
WING	– Grey squirrel tail
TOPPING	– Golden pheasant crest
HEAD	– Black

HAIR-WING WADDINGTON

MOUNT	– Waddington code V1B
HOOK	– Partridge Out-Point Treble code X1BR
THREAD	– Black
BODY	– Black wool
RIB	– Gold oval
WING	– Crimson and purple bucktail
HEAD	– Black

COLLIE DOG

TUBE	– Brass
HOOK	– Partridge Out-Point Treble code X1BR
THREAD	– Black
WING	– Long black hair collie dog, goat or yak
	– Pearl Lureflash
HEAD	– Black

HAIR-WING MEDICINE

HOOK	– Partridge Wilson Dry Fly code 01 size 14–4
THREAD	– Red
BODY	– Silver tinsel
RIB	– Silver oval
HACKLE	– Pale blue cock
WING	– Mixed white and black goat

ORANGE BADGER

HOOK	– Partridge Double code P size 4/0
THREAD	– Black
TAIL	– Golden pheasant crest
BODY	– Orange floss
RIB	– Gold tinsel
HACKLE	– Hot orange cock
WING	– Badger
HEAD	– Black

SUNK LURE

HOOK	– Partridge Wilson Dry Fly code 01
	– Two hooks in tandem size 14–10
THREAD	– Red
BODIES	– Silver tinsel
RIB	– Silver oval
HACKLE	– Pale blue cock
WING	– Mixed bucktail yellow, blue and purple
HEAD	– Red

Plate 14
SMALL SALMON AND SEA TROUT FLIES

MUNRO KILLER

HOOK	– Partridge Salmon Double code P size 10–2
THREAD	– Black
TAG	– Gold wire or oval
TAIL	– Golden pheasant crest and ibis sub

MUNRO KILLER   *continued*
BODY	– Black floss
RIB	– Gold oval
THROAT HACKLE	– Orange cock and blue guinea fowl
WING	– Grey squirrel tail dyed yellow
HEAD	– Black

TUBE COPPER
TUBE	– Copper – heavy
HOOK	– Partridge Out-Point Treble code X1BL size 12–8
BODY	– None
WING	– Mixed bucktail crimson and purple
HEAD	– Black

LONG SHANK TREBLE
HOOK	– Partridge Sea Trout Treble code CS18 size 12–16
THREAD	– Black
TAG	– Silver wire and fluorescent green floss
BODY	– Black floss
RIB	– Silver wire
WING	– Mixed badger hair, yellow and magenta bucktail
HEAD	– Badger

MUNRO TUBE ALUMINIUM
TUBE	– Aluminium – light
HOOK	– Partridge Out-Point Treble code X1LB size 12–8
BODY	– None
WING	– Mixed bucktail – yellow, orange and black
HEAD	– Black

TREBLE
HOOK	– Partridge Treble code X2B size 10–6
HACKLES	– Red, yellow and badger hen

WEE DOUBLE
HOOK	– Partridge Salmon Double code P size 12–8
THREAD	– Black
TAG	– Silver wire
BODY	– Fluorescent yellow floss
RIB	– Silver wire
HACKLE	– Black cock
WING	– Purple crystal hair
HEAD	– Black

Plate 15
SALMON SHRIMPS/PRAWNS

SHANKS'S PURPLE SHRIMP
HOOK	– Partridge Barleet code CS10 size 6
THREAD	– Red
TAG	– Silver oval
TAIL HACKLE	– Golden pheasant breast feather dyed purple
REAR BODY	– Amber antron
REAR RIB	– Silver oval or wire
MIDDLE HACKLE	– Hot orange hen
FRONT BODY	– Black wool
FRONT RIB	– Silver oval or wire
FRONT HACKLE	– Purple cock
EYES	– Jungle cock
HEAD	– Red

SHANKS'S STINCHAR STOAT'S TAIL SHRIMP

HOOK	– Partridge Double code P size 10–4
THREAD	– Black
TAG	– Silver oval or wire
TAIL HACKLE	– Golden pheasant breast feather dyed black
REAR BODY	– Fluorescent hot orange wool
REAR RIB	– Silver oval or wire
MIDDLE HACKLE	– Hot orange hen
FRONT BODY	– Black wool
FRONT RIB	– Silver oval or wire
FRONT HACKLE	– Black cock
EYES	– Jungle cock
HEAD	– Black

ALLY'S SHRIMP

HOOK	– Partridge Double code P size 10–4
THREAD	– Red
ANTENNAE	– Orange bucktail
REAR BODY	– Red floss
EYES	– Golden pheasant tippet
FRONT BODY	– Black floss
RIB	– Silver oval or wire
HACKLE	– Orange cock
HEAD	– Red

STANDARD SHRIMP

HOOK	– Partridge Double code P size 10–4
THREAD	– Red
TAG	– Silver oval or wire
TAIL HACKLE	– Golden pheasant red breast
REAR BODY	– Yellow wool
REAR RIB	– Silver oval or wire
MIDDLE HACKLE	– Orange or yellow hen
FRONT BODY	– Black wool
FRONT RIB	– Silver oval or wire
FRONT HACKLE	– Badger cock
EYES	– Jungle cock
HEAD	– Red

REALISTIC SHRIMP/PRAWN

HOOK	– Partridge Double code P size 10–4
THREAD	– Red
ANTENNAE	– Orange bucktail
HEAD	– Golden pheasant breast dyed hot orange
EYES	– Black beads
BODY	– Hot orange seal sub
BODY HACKLE	– Hot orange cock
BACK AND TAIL	– Orange flexibody
RIB	– Gold oval

SIMPLIFIED GENERAL PRACTITIONER

HOOK	– Partridge Double code P size 10–4
THREAD	– Red
ANTENNAE	– Orange bucktail
BODY	– Orange seal sub
RIB	– Gold oval or wire
BODY HACKLE	– Orange cock
EYES	– Golden pheasant tippet
BACK	– Golden pheasant breast feather
HEAD	– Red

BUMBLE SHRIMP
MATERIALS IDENTICAL TO PURPLE SHRIMP
MOUNT   – Waddington code V1B
                               – Jungle cock optional
TAIL HACKLE   – Tied as collar
MIDDLE AND FRONT
HACKLES   – Wound along body

SB PATTERNS – Vary patterns with weighted goldheads, deer hair wings and heads, marabou tails, Lureflash, Daddy Long Legs and hopper legs

STANDARD PATTERN	THREAD Generally colour of dubbing material	TAILS Front and back – fluorescent floss – very small	UNDERBODY Tinsel, lurex glue/varnish on top	RIBBING Wire – perhaps oval on large sizes	BODY Seal fur sub mixed with pinch of hare to mellow the shade	COCK HACKLE May be omitted or 2 turns before soft hackle or Palmered	SOFT HACKLE Usually covert wing feather
1 MIDGE	BLACK	WHITE	BLUE	SILVER	BLACK & HARE	BLACK	GREY MALLARD
2 CONNEMARA BLACK	BLACK	YELLOW	GOLD	GOLD	BLACK & HARE	BLACK	GROUSE
3 VIVA	BLACK	GREEN	GREEN	GOLD	BLACK & HARE	BLACK	WATER HEN
4 ZULU	BLACK	RED	RED	SILVER	BLACK & HARE	BLACK	CROW
5 DONEGAL BLUE	WHITE	WHITE	SILVER	SILVER	LIGHT BLUE & HARE	MED BLUE DUN	WATER HEN
6 IRON BLUE DUN	RED	ORANGE	BLUE	COPPER	PURPLE & MOLE	DARK BLUE DUN	BROWN PARTRIDGE
7 WOODCOCK & HARE'S EAR	YELLOW	YELLOW	GOLD	GOLD	HARE	NATURAL RED	WOODCOCK
8 HARE'S EAR	YELLOW	YELLOW	PEARL	GOLD	HARE & WHITE	NATURAL RED	GREY MALLARD
9 WOODCOCK & YELLOW	YELLOW	YELLOW	GOLD	GOLD	YELLOW & HARE	GINGER	WOODCOCK

SB PATTERNS – Vary patterns with weighted goldheads, deer hair wings and heads, marabou tails, Lureflash, Daddy Long Legs and hopper legs

STANDARD PATTERN	THREAD Generally colour of dubbing material	TAILS Front and back – fluorescent floss – very small	UNDERBODY Tinsel, lurex glue/varnish on top	RIBBING Wire – perhaps oval on large sizes	BODY Seal fur sub mixed with pinch of hare to mellow the shade	COCK HACKLE May be omitted or 2 turns before soft hackle or Palmered	SOFT HACKLE Usually covert wing feather
10 GROUSE & ORANGE	RED	ORANGE	GOLD	COPPER	ORANGE & HARE	GINGER	GROUSE
11 SOLDIER PALMER	RED	RED	GOLD	GOLD	RED & HARE	RED	GROUSE
12 GROUSE & CLARET	RED	RED	RED	GOLD	CLARET & HARE	CLARET	GROUSE
13 MARCH BROWN	RED	ORANGE	GOLD	COPPER	BROWN & HARE	BROWN	BROWN PARTRIDGE
14 GREEN PETER	YELLOW	ORANGE	GOLD	GOLD	OLIVE & HARE	OLIVE	BROWN PARTRIDGE
15 SOOTY OLIVE	BLACK	ORANGE	GOLD	GOLD	DARK OLIVE & HARE	DARK OLIVE	GROUSE
16 TRIDENT	YELLOW	YELLOW	GOLD	GOLD	REAR HARE FRONT BLACK	NATURAL RED	BLUE JAY
17 WOODCOCK & MIXED	YELLOW	ORANGE	GOLD	GOLD	REAR YELLOW FRONT RED	NATURAL RED	WOODCOCK

Bibliography

Almy, Gerald. *Tying and Fishing Terrestrials*. Stackpole Books 1978

Buckland, John. *The Pocket Guide to Trout and Salmon Flies*. Mitchell Beazley 1986

Clarke, Brian and Goddard, John. *The Trout and the Fly: a New Approach*. Ernest Benn 1980

Collyer, David. *Fly-Dressing II*. David and Charles 1981

Falkus, Hugh. *Sea Trout Fishing Revised Second Edition*. H. F. and G. Witherby 1981

Falkus, Hugh. *Salmon Fishing A Practical Guide*. H. F. and G. Witherby 1984

Fogg, Roger. *The Art of the Wet Fly*. A and C Black 1979

Fogg, Roger. *Stillwater Dry Fly Fishing*. A and C Black 1985

Goddard, John. *Trout Fly Recognition*. A and C Black 1979

Goddard, John. *The Super Flies of Still Water*. Ernest Benn 1977

Harris, Graeme and Morgan, Moc. *Successful Sea Trout Angling*. Blandford Press 1989

Jennings, Preston J. *A Book of Trout Flies*. Crown Publishers Inc., New York 1970

Jorgensen, Poul. *Salmon Flies Their Character, Style and Dressing*. Stackpole Books 1978

Kingsmill-Moore, T. C. *A Man May Fish*. Colin Smythe 1983

Knowles, Derek. *Salmon on a Dry Fly*. H. F. and G. Witherby 1987

Migel, J. Michael (editor). *The Masters On The Dry Fly*.
   J. B. Lippincott Company, Philadelphia and New York 1977

Little, Crawford. *Success With Salmon*. David and Charles 1988

Lapsley, Peter. *The Bankside Book of Stillwater Trout Flies*. A and C Black 1978

Maunsel, G. W. *The Fisherman's Vade Mecum*. A and C Black 1977

Overfield, T. Donald. *G. E. M. Skues: The Way of a Man with a Trout*. Ernest Benn 1977

Overfield, T. Donald. *Famous Flies and their Originators*. A and C Black 1972

Parsons, John. *Deceiving Trout, The Flytier's Art, An International Guide*.
   Airlife Publishing 1988

Price, S. D. (Taff). *Rough Stream Trout Flies*. A and C Black 1976

Price, Taff. *Fly Patterns: an International Guide*. Ward Lock 1986

Pryce-Tannatt, T. E. *How to Dress Salmon Flies*. A and C Black 1977

Sawyer, Frank. *Nymphs and the Trout*. A and C Black 1970

Stewart, Tom. *Two Hundred Popular Flies*. A and C Black 1979

Williams, A. Courtney. *A Dictionary of Trout Flies*. A and C Black 1973

Walker, Richard. *Fly Dressing Innovations*. Ernest Benn 1974

Walker, Richard. *Modern Fly Dressings*. Ernest Benn 1980

Waddington, Richard. *Catching Salmon*. David and Charles 1978

Veniard, John and Downs, Donald. *Fly-tying Problems and their Answers*. A and C Black 1977

Veniard, John. *Fly-Dressing Materials*. A and C Black 1977

Key to Plates

PALMER –
GROUSE &
CLARET

STANDARD –
VIVA

GOLDHEAD
LURE –
GROUSE &
ORANGE

EMERGER/
DRY
WOODCOCK
&
YELLOW

PLATE 2

BLACK
&
SILVER

GOLDEN
OLIVE

MAGENTA
&
RED

COPPER
&
ORANGE

PLATE 3

BLACK &
PEACOCK
SPIDER

BLACK
KE-HE

WORM
FLY

PEACOCK
STICK
FLY

GOAT'S
TOE

PLATE 4

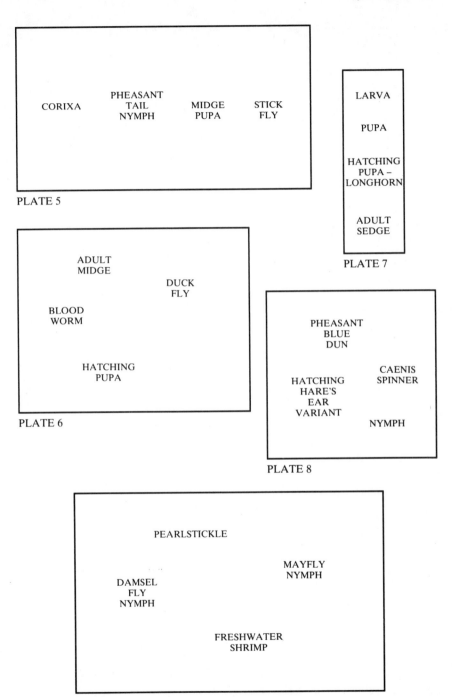

CORIXA   PHEASANT   MIDGE   STICK
           TAIL   PUPA   FLY
           NYMPH

PLATE 5

LARVA

PUPA

HATCHING
PUPA –
LONGHORN

ADULT
SEDGE

PLATE 7

ADULT
MIDGE
                    DUCK
                    FLY

BLOOD
WORM

       HATCHING
       PUPA

PLATE 6

PHEASANT
BLUE
DUN
                    CAENIS
HATCHING   SPINNER
HARE'S
EAR
VARIANT
                    NYMPH

PLATE 8

PEARLSTICKLE

                    MAYFLY
                    NYMPH

DAMSEL
FLY
NYMPH

       FRESHWATER
       SHRIMP

PLATE 9

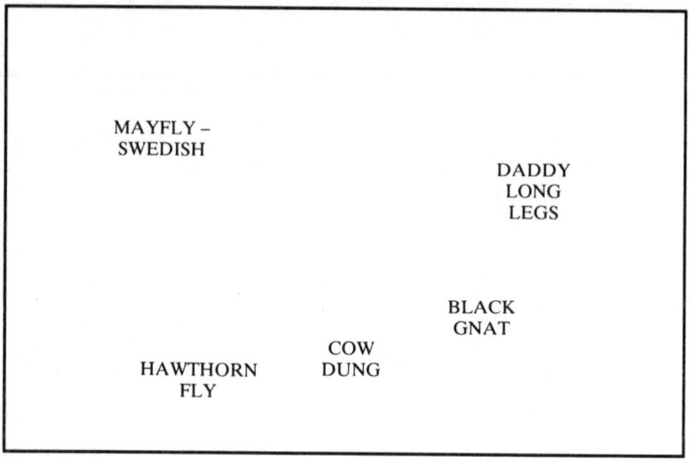

MAYFLY –
SWEDISH

DADDY
LONG
LEGS

BLACK
GNAT

COW
DUNG

HAWTHORN
FLY

PLATE 10

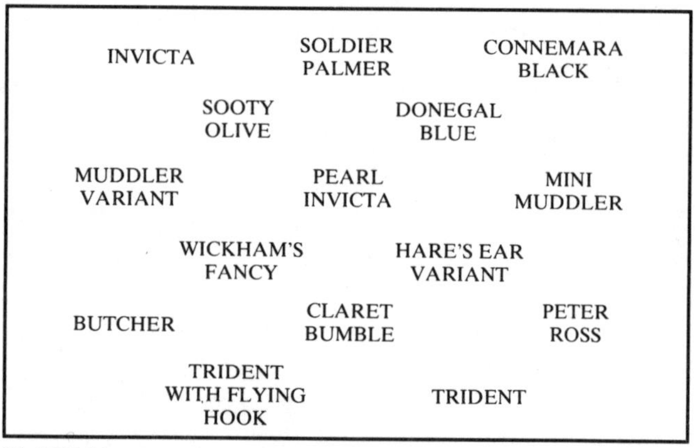

INVICTA   SOLDIER   CONNEMARA
                  PALMER   BLACK

SOOTY   DONEGAL
OLIVE   BLUE

MUDDLER   PEARL   MINI
VARIANT   INVICTA   MUDDLER

WICKHAM'S   HARE'S EAR
FANCY   VARIANT

BUTCHER   CLARET   PETER
                  BUMBLE   ROSS

TRIDENT
WITH FLYING   TRIDENT
HOOK

PLATE 11

JACK
FROST

JERSEY
HERD

MONTANA
NYMPH

BLACK
CAT'S
WHISKER

WHISKY
FLY

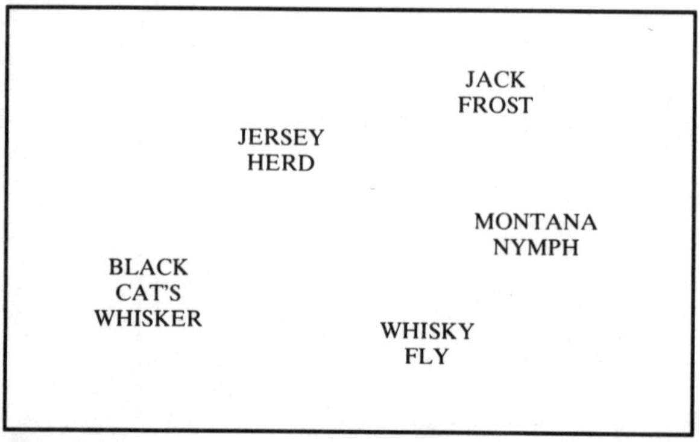

PLATE 12

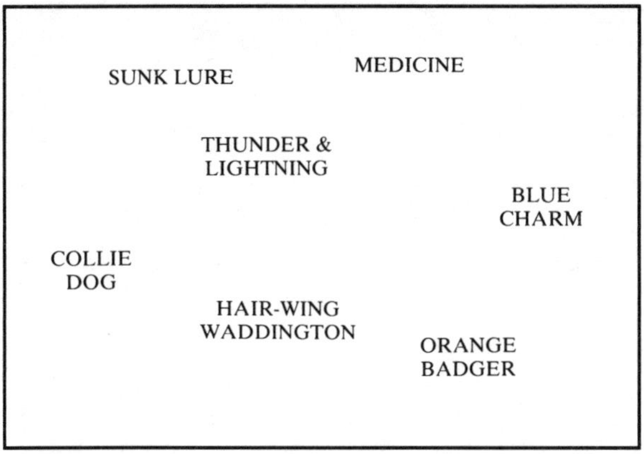

SUNK LURE   MEDICINE

THUNDER &
LIGHTNING

BLUE
CHARM

COLLIE
DOG

HAIR-WING
WADDINGTON

ORANGE
BADGER

PLATE 13

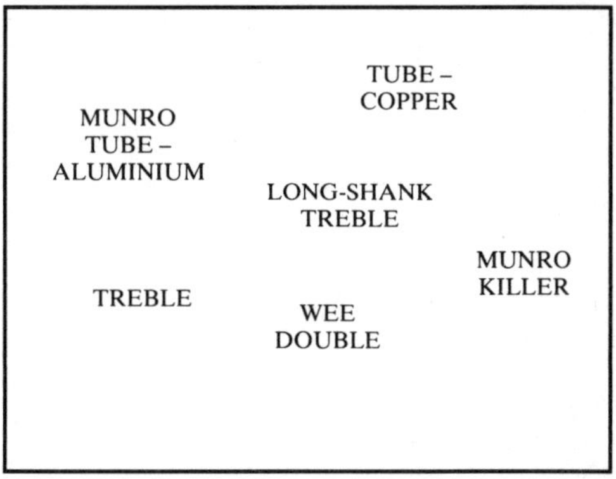

TUBE –
COPPER

MUNRO
TUBE –
ALUMINIUM

LONG-SHANK
TREBLE

MUNRO
KILLER

TREBLE

WEE
DOUBLE

PLATE 14

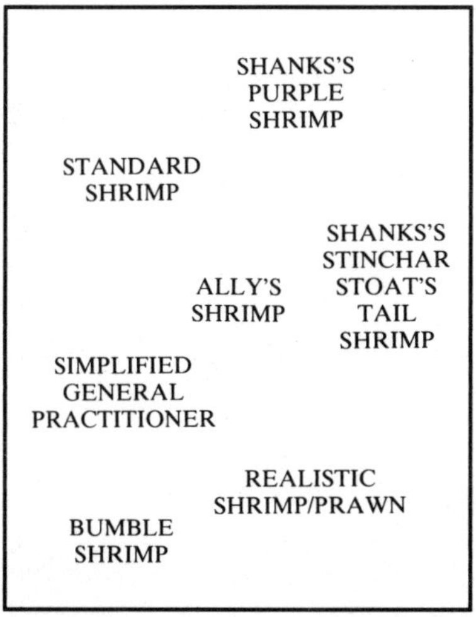

SHANKS'S
PURPLE
SHRIMP

STANDARD
SHRIMP

SHANKS'S
STINCHAR
ALLY'S   STOAT'S
SHRIMP   TAIL
SHRIMP

SIMPLIFIED
GENERAL
PRACTITIONER

REALISTIC
SHRIMP/PRAWN

BUMBLE
SHRIMP

PLATE 15

Index